# THE
# SOURDOUGH
# SCHOOL
# SWEET BAKING

Vanessa Kimbell

# THE SOURDOUGH SCHOOL SWEET BAKING

## NOURISHING THE GUT & THE MIND

Photography by Nassima Rothacker

Kyle Books

To my Alastair. My love.
Just you and me sitting in a tree...
Wife
x

An Hachette UK Company
www.hachette.co.uk

First published in the Great Britain in 2020 by **Kyle Books**, an imprint of Kyle Cathie Ltd
Carmelite House
50 Victoria Embankment
London EC4Y 0DZ
www.octopusbooksusa.com

Distributed in the US by
Hachette Book Group
1290 Avenue of the Americas
4th and 5th Floors
New York, NY 10104

Distributed in Canada by
Canadian Manda Group
664 Annette St.
Toronto, Ontario,
Canada M6S 2C8

Editorial Director **Judith Hannam**
Publisher **Joanna Copestick**
Copy Editor **Tara O'Sullivan**
Editor **Jenny Dye**
Design **Helen Bratby**
Photography **Nassima Rothacker**
Stylist **Michael James**
Cover illustration **Claire Harrup**
Production **Emily Noto**

The Sourdough School is certified organic by the Soil Association. All ingredients mentioned in the book should be organic.

ISBN 978-0-85783-909-1

A CIP catalogue record for this book is available from the British Library.

Printed and bound in China

10 9 8 7 6 5 4 3 2

# Contents

# Foreword
# by Professor Tim Spector

Just five years ago if someone said to you that they were writing a book about sourdough bread and mental health, you would have thought they needed psychiatric help. Today nobody is laughing as the latest science tells us that microbes are the key link between food and the health of our minds and bodies. The science of the microbiome is only a decade old—but it is probably the most exciting and fast-moving field of medicine. Food as medicine was big at the time of the ancient Greeks and slowly lost its influence, but it is having a major renaissance. This is partly the result of the new scientific discoveries, but also a backlash against the influence of the pharmaceutical industry that has been pushing expensive drugs of reducing benefit and increasing side effects on us. As the pharmaceutical companies are now giving way to the increasing financial and political power of the dozen global food companies that supply 70 per cent of our food, many of us are rejecting the highly processed products on offer and want to find out more about traditional or artisan foods and how to make them ourselves.

There is now increasingly good evidence that switching to a healthy diet is as good as the average effect of an anti-depressant. Traditional breadmaking using whole grains and natural yeast starters is at the heart of a good healthy diet, providing crucial amounts of fibre that most of us lack as well as other nutrients and gut-friendly chemicals. The microbes that create the gas that makes the bread die in the process of baking. Although some early research indicates dead microbes can provide some benefit to humans, this is still speculative. But just the act of preparing the dough and baking may itself confer unexpected health benefits. Every sourdough baker will carry healthy bacteria and yeast on their hands which will be unique to them, making every starter unique in the composition of microbes. There is anecdotal evidence that bakers are on average healthier than their peers and some of this may be due to the benefits of manual work as well as their regular contact with friendly microbes leading to a more diverse gut community.

As everyone has a unique set of gut microbes, and even identical twins only share around a third of them, it is hard to define the perfect healthy gut community known as the gut microbiome. Nevertheless, researchers around the world like myself, have consistently found that the number of different species or microbiome diversity is the common factor that separates people with health problems from those without. In a study of 11,000 samples from combining the British and American Gut projects we found that the most important factor determining high gut microbe diversity was not whether you were vegan or gluten free— but how many different plants you eat per week.

We found that diversity increased steadily until you got to 30 plant varieties weekly. To many people this sounds a challenge, but as Vanessa explains in this book, by plants we also mean not just broccoli but every type of nut, seed, grain, herb, and berry. This makes the task of feeding your gut microbes optimally much more interesting and exciting than just drinking kale smoothies.

This book is a much-needed, unique, and very practical guide to how you can use the new knowledge of the gut microbes to improve your health as well as developing and expanding your skills in the kitchen. Once you understand the art of fermenting foods you are in a privileged position to grasp how microbes work inside your own body and how important it is to keep them happy. This book is packed with novel tips on how to enhance every dish you make in a way that will be great for the health of your microbes, and you will learn all about their favourite foods like special types of fibre, pro- and pre-biotics and the amazing world of polyphenols. On the journey with this book you will discover many tasty new dishes and combinations enriching your body, mind and microbes—so enjoy!

**Tim Spector MB MSC FRCP FSB FMedSci**
**Professor of Genetic Epidemiology**
**Kings College London**
**Author of** *The Diet Myth* **and** *Spoon Fed*
**@timspector**

'the latest science tells us that microbes are the key link between food and the health of our minds and bodies'

# Introduction

This book tells the story of how we have evolved with symbiotic microbes at our core, how we lost our way of eating, and how we can find our way back again. In this story you are the hero: because reading and baking from this book isn't just baking. It is an act of defiance and beautiful disruption. But before I tell you more about that, let's start at the beginning.

## Who are we really?

We evolved symbiotically with a collective of microbes at the heart of our digestive system to become the complex sentient beings we are today. Although we are only just beginning to understand the full extent to which we are connected to the microbial world, we now have irrefutable evidence that the health and diversity of our gut microbiome affects both mood and cognitive function. These microbes are on our hands, in the soil and in the biosphere. They are the foundations of our world, and finally we have the scientific understanding that explains how our food, hearts, and minds are inextricably linked, not just by consciousness, but by a collective of powerful microbes that go all the way to our creation and back again.

There is emerging evidence that in the West, our biomes have, on average, less than 50 per cent of the diversity we once had, compared to hunter-gatherer tribes such as the Hadza Tribe in Tanzania. Some scientists are even discussing extinction-level loss of microbial diversity.

## Is everything you understand about baking wrong?

While this book has incredibly delicious recipes to bake and eat, it is not a book about baking. This is a book about understanding. I will share some of the most detailed knowledge of the connection between our food, gut microbiome and potential impact on mental health to date, both in the book and at the Sourdough School. This is an insight into the future of our food.

## Why focus on mental health

The workshops at my Sourdough School are centred around the relationship between wellness, grain fermentation and the gut microbiome, because our gut health has been linked to so many areas of health. In fact, almost all non-communicable diseases have been linked to gut health, from diabetes and obesity to autoimmune conditions, such as arthritis, and neurodegenerative diseases, such as Alzheimer's. Although physical and mental health are not separate, together they are a vast topic, so in this book I have chosen to focus on mental health and baking to feed the people we love. Knowing how what we eat can affect our mood is one thing, but understanding how to apply this knowledge in our homes is quite another. My personal definition of being in good mental health is to care: because when we stop caring, we are no longer empathic, and we self-destruct.

## Exactly what is meant by mental health?

According to the World Health Organisation (WHO), good mental health is "a state of well-being in which every individual realizes his or her own potential, can cope with the normal stresses of life, can work productively and fruitfully, and is able to make a contribution to her or his community". In modern society, there are not only epidemic numbers of people suffering from anxiety, depression, and stress, but also a growing number of people suffering from severe disorders such as schizophrenia.

It is now estimated that over 40 per cent of people visiting their GP in the UK are reporting mental health issues. We have to take mental health seriously. Statistics show that people with mental health disorders are more likely to have a significantly increased risk of type 2 diabetes and even some cancers, and are six times more likely to die from cardiovascular disease (even if they are aged between 25 and 44 years).

## Getting your hands busy

There is a huge body of evidence to show that physically making something or learning a new skill has a rewiring effect that disrupts patterns in the brain. This has been found to help lower stress and anxiety levels. Baking is about taking time for yourself, but it equally it is about sharing and making a social connection. Again, the evidence of this being good for mental health is extremely well reported.

## Modern baking – a tragic loop

The fact that baking has the potential to be good for the soul is enough to get me into the kitchen. Sharing a treat is an expression of compassion, and all home-baked goods avoid the multitudes of preservatives and additives (including emulsifiers, which have been proven to reduce gut microbial diversity) found in commercial baked goods. That said, there is a tragic irony in expressing love for someone or cheering yourself up with something that is made with high levels of refined flour and sugar, unwittingly exacerbating the malnourishment of a Western gut microbiome.

## Why should you be concerned about our food system?

This is a book about comfort food, but it will not always be comfortable to read. I will be challenging your ideas about baking, because our diet is one of the major factors in the devolution of our cognitive function and in the erosion of our collective relationship with each other and our planet. To continue as we are now is to destroy the symbiotic relationship we evolved with: a micro-destruction. The consequences of continuing to starve our gut of the essential fibre we need will be just as devastating as the macro-destruction taking place in our global environment. We must address both if we are to survive as a species.

## How what you eat could change the way you feel

An incredible body of evidence is emerging in a new field of research into food and mental health, with pioneering scientists such as Felice Jacka and her team at the Food and Mood Centre leading the way. One of Felice's findings was that women who ate higher levels of wholegrains, fruit and vegetables were less likely to suffer from depression. John Cryan, a neuropharmacologist and gut microbiome expert from the University College Cork, has been uncovering evidence that certain probiotics (see page 62) have a positive effect on mood. We are still learning about the full impact of the way we eat on the way we feel. What we do finally have, though, is a base on which to understand both the microbes in our guts and the role of fermentation in baking. We can apply this evidence to the way we bake, and in so doing, discover the importance of grain diversity and our biosphere, Earth. I will be going into all these details, with evidence about how the way we approach our baking can nurture our gut microbes. I'll be exploring the studies about how our cakes, bakes and breads may even modulate the microbes that contribute to mental health and brain function. It has taken years to bring the research together, and waiting for more evidence is frustrating, so all the sources used in our research (over 300 studies) and the most up-to-date resources for further reading are shared on our website.

# Where do we go from here?

Nourishment is the starting point for change. You will learn how you can optimize your mental health by changing the way you bake. All the recipes in this book are "diversity bakes". A robust gut microbiome is associated with better mental health. This is achieved through using a diversity of ingredients. Challenging a system that is heavily based on industrially produced foods that are high in refined carbohydrates and sugar is not only about knowledge, but achievable action. To create, bake, and nourish is an enjoyable and anarchistic approach to change.

# But I'm not ill ...

Given that a combination of poor diet and poor mental health are the leading causes of mortality and morbidity worldwide, we cannot wait for the medical profession to lead. Indeed, by the time you get to the doctor, much of the damage is already done. The Institute of Medicine (now known as the National Academy of Medicine) uncovered that research can take up to 17 years to reach our local surgeries. So, before you dismiss the concept of eating for mental health, think carefully. Perhaps rather than wait until we become unwell, we should use the opportunity of feeling well to stay well.

# In the end ...

Baking is essentially a way to express love, the most powerful feeling in the world. It is not words that you will remember about a moment in time, but the way you felt. Your state of mind defines who you are and your place in the world. Baking is no longer just an indulgence. It is a radical act that will empower you to understand how to eat co-operatively with your gut microbiome. This will give you the power to live the most beautiful (and delicious) life possible.

Love, bake, nourish.
Vanessa x

Baker Michael James, author of *The Tivoli Road Baker* and the amazing guest stylist for this book.

# Notes

# The gut microbiome & mood

The secret is that we are symbiotic. It's easy to imagine that, as humans, we exist on our own, but in fact we are in a symbiotic relationship with microbes. The earth has its own microbiome, the soil is teeming with billions of microbes, and our skin and entire digestive and reproductive systems have their own microbiomes too. Once you understand this relationship, you have the knowledge, and with this knowledge comes great responsibility; because if you are well, everything is more beautiful.

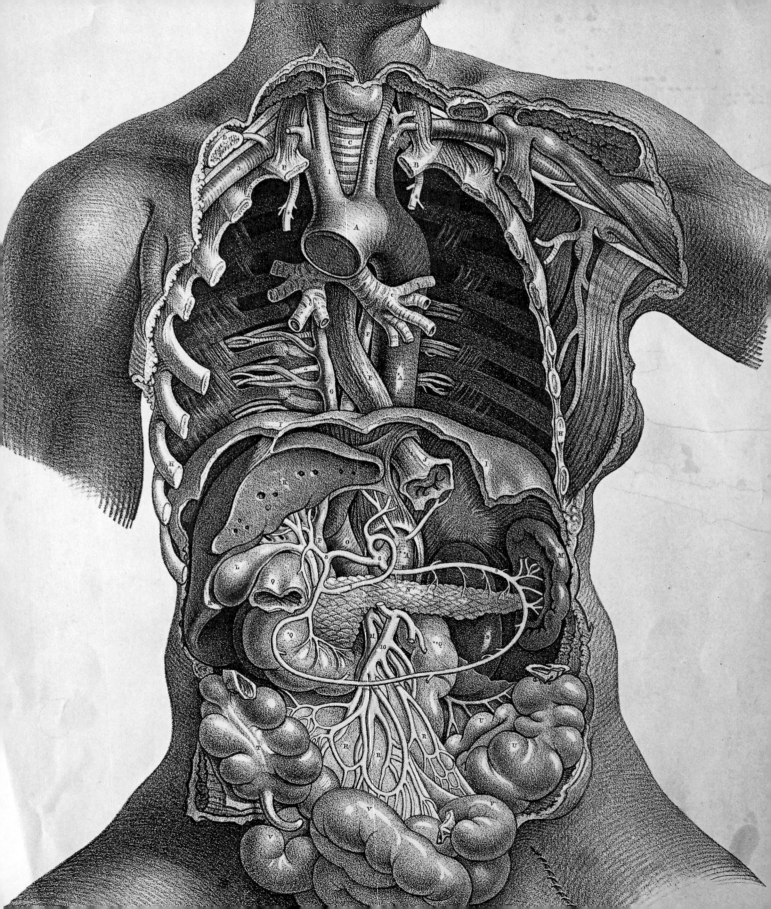

# It's not just gut health

Even as I am writing, there are new studies being published on the gut–brain connection. The gut has proved to be a key link, drawing us together from every scientific discipline and all parts of the wellness world, because this collective of microorganisms is the indisputable connection between all aspects of physical and mental health.

Once we understand the role of the gut, we have the fundamental knowledge needed to enjoy eating well so that we can feel well. I say that with all the emphasis I can muster: so that we can *feel* well. Eating to support our gut microbiome means we can feel well on both a physical and an emotional level. We're talking about feeling well, feeling alert, feeling energetic, feeling full of life.

So, the formulas and techniques in this book will take you far beyond baking. It is about wellbeing. Not just your own, but the wellbeing of those you bake for.

If you are not into the scientific details, feel free to skip this entire section. I totally get just wanting to get on and bake; but there are millions of recipes in the world. The magical thing about this book is not in the recipes, it is in the application of this knowledge. It is this approach that will change the way you think about baking.

**MICROBIAL DIVERSITY** is an important indicator of balance and stability in the ecosystem of the body. Greater bacterial diversity deters pathogens, indicates complementary activities by different microbes and ensures that other bacteria can take over important health-promoting tasks if something happens to a specific species.

## What is the gut microbiome?

The gut microbiota (also known as gut flora) is the name given to the bacteria, viruses, yeasts, and archaea that inhabit our digestive system. Over the past decade or so, the gene sequencing techniques that were developed to map the human genome in the early 2000s have been applied to the human gut microbiota. The reality is we're still at the very frontier of understanding how these microbes interact and their roles and individual nuances. We are beginning to identify the foods that can support a healthy and diverse microbial community, which in turn is linked to good health (Riaz Rajoka et al., 2017). It's these foods that we will be focusing on in the sweet sourdough recipes.

The human colon (large intestine) is home to trillions of bacterial cells, far more in fact than we have in the rest of our body. This ecosystem is called the gut microbiome and it lives in harmony with us, the hosts. Our gut bacteria perform many essential tasks, not just breaking down dietary fibre into beneficial substances, but also regulating the immune system, preventing inflammation, and deterring pathogenic bacteria from making us sick. (I'll talk more about this when we look at short-chain fatty acids on page 20.)

# Types of microbes

There are many different types of microbes, and the terminology can be a bit confusing. But don't worry, it's actually pretty simple when it's explained clearly. There are divisions of microbes (known as phyla, the plural of phylum) that share similar structures and traits. There are four dominant bacterial phyla in the human gut. They are Firmicutes, Bacteroidetes, Actinobacteria and Proteobacteria. Inside each phylum there are different genera (the plural of genus), and finally, there are species, a subdivision of genera. So, a phylum might be home to "good" and "opportunistic" bacteria, while a genus refers to smaller groups within that phylum, and species to one specific type of bacteria within that.

I try to avoid the term "bad" bacteria, because this microscopic ecosystem is far more complex than that. Potentially bad bacteria are often called "opportunistic". That's because if they colonize the gut, they can disrupt our body's normal processes and, in some cases, make us sick. In the same vein, some bacteria can be good, but if there are too many or too few compared to the rest of the community, this can also cause issues.

What has become clear in recent years is that our sugar-heavy, fibre-poor, low-diversity, industrialized diet is one of the things responsible for the reduced diversity in our gut microbiome. An impoverished gut microbiota leaves us vulnerable to gut dysbiosis (see below). Throughout the book we'll be looking at how sourdough baking can help enhance our gut microbiome. We'll explore how a long, slow fermentation facilitates the bioavailability of the nutrients that are key in helping to nurture the gut microbiome, and we'll look at ways to increase dietary diversity through fermented and fibre-rich foods.

When your gut microbiome is unbalanced, we call this "dysbiosis", and it can cause a wide range of issues, such as digestive problems, cramps, diarrhea, constipation and gas. It is also a source of chronic inflammation that is linked to a wide range of illnesses, including gluten intolerances, food allergies, autoimmune disorders and mental health issues. Fortunately, prebiotic substances in your food, like dietary fibre and polyphenols, are known to nourish helpful bacteria that are able to balance the gut microbiome and help restore health. Later in the book we will be looking at the kind of prebiotic fibres we should be eating and discovering which microbes they nourish.

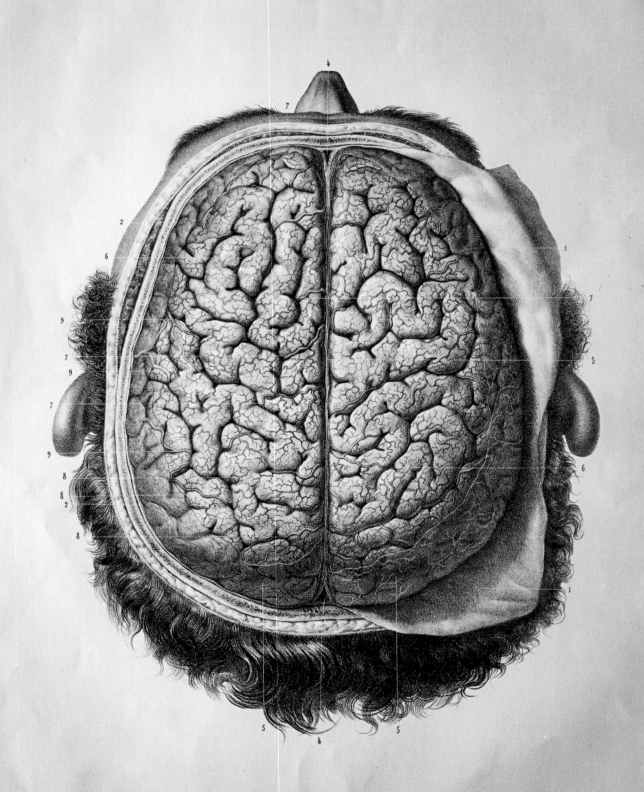

# Gut–brain communication

Your gut is home to the enteric nervous system, which fires off signals to your digestive tract and tells it when to do everything. And even though it works without you having to lift a finger, it's still connected to your brain by a vagus nerve, so your gut and brain are constantly communicating about what's for dinner and whether you feel a bit gassy.

Your bacteria can even get in on the action too, because there are lots of nerve fibres embedded throughout your gut lining. They produce and encourage the production of many molecules that allow them to interact with you. And that means that when you feel stressed, your bacteria can too. It also means that if your gut microbiome is unbalanced, your brain might experience stress. (Foster, Rinaman and Cryan, 2017)

## Key to mood: serotonin and GABA

### THE "HAPPY HORMONE"

It's really important to provide bacteria with the fibre they need to do their job, as they play a role in managing mood with other molecules. Serotonin, known as "the happy hormone", is produced by bacteria in the gut and works as a neurotransmitter for the nervous system. Serotonin influences the way you feel on many levels, including regulating mood, reducing appetite, and helping to establish a feeling of well-being. Altered levels of peripheral serotonin have been associated with irritable bowel syndrome (IBS), cardiovascular disease, and osteoporosis.

Low levels have also been linked with depression. It is produced in both the intestines and the brain: it is estimated that 90 per cent of the body's serotonin is made in the digestive tract. The short-chain fatty acids (SCFAs, see page 20) made by our microbes actually modulate serotonin production by the cells in our gut, so we have it at optimum levels in the body. It is important to note that serotonin cannot cross the blood–brain barrier, so any serotonin that is used in the brain must first be produced inside the brain.

### REDUCING ANXIETY

There's also GABA (otherwise known as gamma-aminobutyric acid), which acts as a relaxant on the brain, mitigating stress reactions conveyed by the nervous system and reducing anxiety. Lactic acid bacteria actually produce it during the fermentation process, including in that of sourdough (Yunes et al., 2016), yogurt and cheese. Probiotic *Lactobacillus*, such as *L. rhamnosus*, as well as *Bifidobacterium*, may even be able to help our body capture GABA, thereby helping reduce anxiety.

## Dopamine

### FEELING GOOD

Another example of the gut being at the centre of mood is an important neurochemical called dopamine, which boosts mood and is involved in regulation of movement, learning, sense of satisfaction, and emotional responses. Dopamine is often referred to as the feel-good neurotransmitter. It is a chemical that facilitates information between neurons. The brain releases it when we do things we like, such as eating or having sex. More than 50 per cent of the body's dopamine lies in the gut. Increasing evidence shows disruption in gut microbiota composition in association with psychiatric disorders, including anxiety and depression. So, as with serotonin, the gut is central to production of the key neurochemicals essential to regulating mood.

# What are prebiotics?

Prebiotics are non-digestible elements, like complex sugars, dietary fibres, and resistant starches in whole foods, mostly from plants and fungi (with a few exceptions). The detailed studies of these are on pages 38–39. They have been attracting a lot of scientific interest in recent years. That's because, even though our body doesn't have the enzymes to break them down, our gut microbes do. Prebiotics go to the large intestine, where our gut microbes break them down into beneficial compounds called short-chain fatty acids (SCFAs). There are eight kinds, but we are most interested in three called butyrate (see below), propionate and acetate.

### INCREASING YOUR BUTYRATE-PRODUCING MICROBES

The recipes in this book are designed to increase numbers of microbes that produce butyrate. Sometimes known as butyric acid, this important short-chain fatty acid (SCFA) helps prevent inflammation and the invasion of pathogenic bacteria. It is one of the main sources of fuel for gut cells, along with two other SCFAs called acetate and propionate. Together, they provide about 15 per cent of the body's energy needs.

Butyrate maintains the gut lining by stimulating the growth of villi. These tiny extrusions on the intestinal wall absorb nutrients. Butyrate also has anti-inflammatory and antioxidant properties, and plays a central role in orchestrating the tight junction protein complexes to control gut barrier function (Jefferson and Adolphus, 2019). In other words, it helps to maintain the integrity of our gut wall, so toxins, metabolites, large food molecules, bacteria and viruses can't get into our body. Your body's ability to produce butyrate depends on the microbes being plentiful in the first place, as well as your gut getting complex carbohydrates. So, the more often you eat these recipes as part of your regular diet, the better your body's ability to make butyrate.

## So, what do SCFAs do? It's more of a question of what don't they do

▶ Short-chain fatty acids have been credited with a range of health benefits, including weight control and reduced risk of colon cancer.
▶ SCFAs provide food that supplies energy to epithelial cells in the large intestine, helping to protect our gut.
▶ SCFAs help to maintain blood sugar levels, meaning that they contribute to keeping blood sugar stable (glucose homeostasis). When it comes to mood, keeping your blood sugar stable is important. Low blood sugar increases levels of cortisol, a hormone associated with stress.
▶ SCFAs help with appetite regulation.
▶ They help the transit of your food through the gut by bulking out stools.
▶ Butyrate is also involved in regulating immune response, and so reducing inflammation.
(Kim, Park and Kim, 2014)

## Starving our microbes

The modern Western diet is exceedingly fibre-poor by historical standards. It contains a paltry 15g fibre daily. The recommended daily allowance (RDA) in the UK is 30g for an adult, but there is evidence that we actually evolved eating close to 10 times that amount of fibre per day. Imagine the devastating effect this lack of fibre has had on our microbiota and our ability to produce SCFAs.

# Mood and microbes: powerful beneficial bacteria in your gut

## Which gut bacteria are key in affecting mood?

The message of this book is to take care of your gut microbes, so that they can take care of you. But exactly which ones should we be looking after? Well, we are trying to keep a balance, along with diversity. It's still early days, but our understanding of how microbes affect the human mood is evolving at a considerable pace. There are more animal studies than human, but the microbes below are the key positive microbes known to modulate mood.

### SYNBIOTICS

The idea of synbiotics is to feed the beneficial probiotics (see page 62) with a source of sustenance in the form of prebiotics, thus improving the survival of the probiotic bacteria in the gut.

### AKKERMANSIA MUCINIPHILA

This species of microbes got its name "muciniphila" because it enjoys munching on mucin, the gel-like substance that lines the intestines. For healthy people, that's a good thing, because it stimulates cells in the gut to produce more mucin. This thickens the lining, helping to preserve the epithelial barrier and prevent inflammation. Studies also show that *Akkermansia* is genetically capable of producing vitamins B1, B2, B3, B5, B6, B7, and B9. These microbes don't just eat mucin, though. They have been shown to feed on polyphenols, which are found in berries; apparently they particularly like cranberries. Studies in mice show that *Akkermansia* plays a role in preventing obesity, type 2 diabetes and inflammation.

### CHRISTENSENELLA

This lesser-known microbe has been shown to play a role in preventing weight gain, and some researchers even consider it a marker of longevity because it has been found in greater relative abundance in people aged over 105 years than in other adults. *Christensenella* is considered to be a heritable microbe because it is often identified in the gut microbiome of related people. It is also more common in people with lower body mass. These bacteria use dietary fibres found in plant foods like fruit, grains and berries to produce SCFAs (page 20).

### BIFIDOBACTERIA: KEY TO MOOD

These probiotic bacteria make up about 90 per cent of our gut microbial ecosystem during our first three years. After this, they drop drastically, but they still actively participate in our gut health. They have been shown to help manage diarrhea associated with enteric (gut) infections and antibiotic use. They also crowd out bad bacteria, such as *C. perfringens* and *C. histolyticum* (Duenas et al., 2015). They may even help reduce several allergic reactions. The *Bifidobacterium* genus of microbes is subdivided into dozens of species, many of which add their own specific probiotic attributes to the gut ecosystem. Even without diving into the details, we know that these microbes produce acetate and lactate, helping to balance the pH of the gut, while nourishing the beneficial bacteria that produce butyrate and SCFAs (see page 20). *Bifidobacterium* produce several vitamins and break down polyphenols to make their antioxidant and anti-inflammatory functions available to the body. These microbes are not just in the gut. They are versatile, and you can find them in live dairy ferments like yogurt and kefir, in which they can produce vitamins B1, B2, B7, B9 and B12, as well as GABA (see page 19). You can nourish the *Bifidobacteria* in your gut with foods rich in polyphenols and certain dietary fibres found in the ingredients used in this book, such as flours from wholegrains, berries, grapes, mangoes, apples and kiwis.

## COPROCOCCUS

These microbes are common in the human gut and perform a variety of functions. They are able to transform a type of prebiotic called "polysaccharides" (complex plant sugars that nourish the gut microbiome) into important short-chain fatty acids that support a healthy gut and prevent inflammation. Recent research indicates that lower levels of *Coprococcus* are found in the gut microbiome of depressed people, suggesting that it plays an important role in modulating the gut–brain axis, and therefore mental health. Lower levels of *Coprococcus* have also been identified in patients with irritable bowel syndrome.

## EUBACTERIUM

This species is one of the gut microbiome's most important producers of butyrate (see page 20). There are several common species of *Eubacterium* in the human gut, some of which can directly break down plant compounds, like pectin in apples, as well as several polyphenols. However, this microbe commonly exists in symbiosis with *Bifidobacterium* (see left). *Bifidobacterium* produce lactate, which *Eubacterium hallii* turn into butyrate. This is known as cross feeding. Resistant starches and prebiotic fibres called arabinoxylans (page 25), have been shown to encourage the abundance of *Eubacterium* in the gut.

## FAECALIBACTERIUM

A common member of the human gut microbiome, the *Faecalibacterium* genus breaks down prebiotic dietary fibres, like pectins and resistant starches, which are found in the fruit and wholegrains used in this book. Out of the many gut bacterial species studied so far, the primary species of this genus, *Faecalibacterium prausnitzii*, is a leading producer of butyrate (see page 20). The presence of *F. prausnitzii* in the gut is considered a marker of intestinal health.

### LACTOBACILLUS: KEY TO MOOD
This genus belongs to the lactic acid bacteria group, known for their probiotic properties. Species of *Lactobacillus* have been shown to have a positive effect on many things, from antibiotic-induced diarrhea to alleviating depression and anxiety and helping with stress resilience and mood disorders. In the kitchen, lactic acid bacteria create an acidic environment in fermented foods, like yogurt, kefir and kimchi, protecting us from invading pathogens. *Lactobacillus* do the same in the gut by producing lactate. By lowering the pH of our colon, they create a friendly environment for good microbes, some of which also turn lactate into butyrate (see page 20). These bacteria are present in cultured dairy and can be nourished in the gut with the wholegrains, pectin and other fibres found in this book's recipes.

## PREVOTELLA

*Prevotella* are common gut microbes that are particularly prominent in the gut microbiome of Amazonian and African tribes, who traditionally eat many hard-to-digest plant fibres, like hemicellulose. They are present in higher abundances in vegetarians, who consume a high-fibre, plant-based diet. *Prevotella* can improve how the body metabolizes sugars in the diet, and controlling the rate of assimilation of carbohydrates and blood sugar is key to mood. One study has shown that *Prevotella* increased in numbers following barley supplementation in the diet, which encouraged interactions and communications between other bacteria involved in breaking down carbohydrates. A balanced gut is a team effort.

## ROSEBURIA

These bacteria are some of the gut ecosystem's most important participants because they produce butyrate (see page 20). *Roseburia* thrive in the beneficial acidic environment created by lactic acid bacteria and *Bifidobacterium*, which acts as a deterrent to pathogens. Culinary traditions like the Mediterranean diet, which is high in fibre, antioxidants and unsaturated fatty acids, have been shown to positively influence the abundance of *Roseburia* in the gut microbiome. In particular, xylans (page 27), a type of dietary fibre found in cereal grains used in the recipes in this book, support the presence of *Roseburia* in the gut.

# How to nourish beneficial bacteria

ONCE YOU UNDERSTAND THAT WE ARE SYMBIOTIC WITH THE MICROBES IN OUR GUT, YOUR WHOLE PERSPECTIVE AS A BAKER CHANGES.

As I began to understand the importance (and needs) of our gut microbes, I began to look differently at the ingredients that I bake with every day. Epidemiological studies show correlation between the consumption of grains and a reduction in many non-communicable diseases including obesity (which is now considered a low-grade systematic inflammatory disease), type 2 diabetes and autoimmune conditions. Eating grains has been shown to modulate the microbes in the gut, but I wanted to know what specifically nourished which microbes. Suddenly, I looked at the ingredients we bake with in a new light, from the perspective of nurturing the gut microbes. In order to understand exactly what our gut microbes needed to thrive, I began researching.

Below is a breakdown of the specific fibres and the positive microbes that we know they feed. If you don't like science, don't worry; the fibre and your microbes still behave in exactly the same way whether or not you know their names or which specific bacteria they nourish!

## How do we influence the balance of beneficial bacteria?

Prebiotics stimulate colonies of good bacteria, like probiotic microbes *Bifidobacterium* and *Lactobacillus*, but they also encourage lesser-known microbes that produce butyrate (page 20). Most prebiotics also directly contribute to improving our digestive health by hastening the transit time of food in our gut and also modulating constipation and diarrhea.

# Exactly what nourishes positive bacteria?

It comes down to increasing both the amount and diversity of fibre and phytochemicals we eat. I've included all of the fibres below in the Botanical Blends on pages 55–57, but it's not enough to just take my word for it. Understanding the reason for diversity will change the way you bake, so this is a summary of the research on the main prebiotic foods that we know increase beneficial bacteria.

### AMYLOPECTIN

This type of resistant starch is commonly found in grains including wheat. It is a prebiotic fibre that nourishes happy bacteria in the gut microbiome. In particular, several strains of probiotic *Bifidobacteria* (see page 22), like *B. infantis*, and *B. longum*, are able to use amylopectin in the gut, thus helping to maintain correct acidity levels, which in turn deter pathogens and attract helpful bacteria (see Synbiotics, page 22). So it makes perfect sense to combine ingredients such as wheat (which contains amylopectin) with the live bacteria found in recipes such as the fermented crème pâtissière (page 75), especially when you consider evidence that probiotic strains of *Bifidobacteria* have recognized properties for alleviating anxiety and reducing inflammation.

### ARABINOXYLAN

A major subtype of hemicellulose, arabinoxylan is found in wholegrain cereals like wheat, especially in the bran. Arabinoxylan has been specifically found to improve blood glucose control in people with poor glucose tolerance. This may be due to the viscosity of this fibre, which prevents all the glucose from being absorbed in the gut, potentially steadying blood sugar levels. It has also been shown to increase levels of probiotic *Bifidobacterium* and decrease colonies of bacteria associated with dysbiosis (see page 16).

### BETA-GLUCAN

Beta-glucan is found in both oats and barley as a complex plant sugar (polysaccharide) that functions as a prebiotic, nourishing the bacteria in our gut so that they can fulfil their health-promoting functions. It is a soluble fibre with gelling properties that has been shown to improve blood glucose control and cholesterol levels. Beta-glucan can contribute to gut microbial health by encouraging the probiotic bacteria *Lactobacillus* and *Bifidobacterium*, which have anti-inflammatory functions, produce nutrients and deter invaders (see pages 22–23). A diet with sufficient beta-glucan can help increase our gut bacteria's production of short-chain fatty acids (page 20).

### CELLULOSE

This long-chain carbohydrate is found in all wholegrains, nuts and seeds, and the skins of some vegetables and fruit. It has been shown that specific gut microbiome traits found in some people (often correlated with gut microbiome-mediated methane production) may confer the ability to break down cellulose and turn it into beneficial short-chain fatty acids. For the rest of us, we know that cellulose can improve bowel movements, because it's a dietary fibre with low potential for fermentation in the gut.

### (WHEAT) DEXTRIN

This hard-to-digest plant fibre moves through our small intestine (where our body absorbs nutrients directly from our food) and travels to our colon. Here it provides a source of food for our gut microbes, which is why it's considered to be a "fermentable" fibre (because bacteria ferment things), and thus prebiotic. It's a soluble fibre, meaning that it absorbs water and has gelling properties, giving it the ability to capture by-products from our metabolism (like cholesterol) and carry them out of the body in the stool. Wheat dextrin has been shown to help stabilise blood sugar, increase micronutrient absorption and regulate the digestive system. Gut bacteria also use it to produce butyrate, propionate and acetate, those lovely short-chain fatty acids that I keep talking about. That's probably because wheat dextrin appeals to those important probiotic bacteria, *Bifidobacterium* and *Lactobacillus* (pages 22–23).

### FERULIC ACID

This makes up about 90 per cent of the polyphenols in wheat and triggers the germination of grains in the soil. Studies in mice show that it can also be broken down in the gut microbiome by *Lactobacillus spp.*, a species of bacteria with probiotic (see page 67) properties. These microbes help balance pH in the gut microbiome, making it attractive to beneficial bacteria and deterring others. It also produces acetate, an important short-chain fatty acid that contributes to gut microbial health. Ferulic acid has antioxidant and anti-inflammatory properties that are important for the body. Research even indicates that it might be beneficial as a form of therapy for Alzheimer's.

### FRUCTO-OLIGOSACCHARIDES

These are complex sugars found in whole plant foods that are not digestible by our body; instead they are broken down by gut microbes. That is why fructo-oligosaccharides (FOS) are a type of prebiotic that are particularly appealing to the probiotic *Bifidobacteria*, which help maintain a healthy gut environment. This prebiotic encourages the production of short-chain fatty acid by our gut microbes and helps to balance the pH in the colon. FOS may also help to regulate body weight by suppressing ghrelin, known as the hunger hormone. In addition to that, FOS have been shown to improve the movement of food through the gut and thus to reduce constipation. FOS can also enhance the absorption of minerals such as calcium, magnesium, iron and zinc. Although mostly found in savoury vegetables, it is also present in the oats and rye that we use as the base of our Botanical Blends (pages 55–57).

### GALACTO-OLIGOSACCHARIDES: A KEY PLAYER

Galacto-oligosaccharides (GOS) are a type of prebiotic complex carbohydrate found in legumes, nuts, rye and seeds. GOS resist our digestive enzymes, travelling through the gastrointestinal tract to the colon, where they are slowly broken down by beneficial bacteria. A type of soluble fibre, they have been shown to stimulate *Bifidobacterium* and *Lactobacillus* growth in the gut microbiome (pages 22–23) and even improve calcium absorption.

### HEMICELLULOSE

Hemicellulose is an insoluble dietary fibre found in the cell walls of plants that has the ability to speed up the movement of food through our gut and bulk up our stool; an important contribution in a world where constipation is a regular and unwanted feature of our everyday lives. Hemicellulose is mainly found in cereal grains, pulses and bran. There are several different types, including arabinoxylan (page 25) and xylan (page 27), which have prebiotic properties.

### INULIN

This fermentable, soluble fibre is—you guessed it—a prebiotic that, even at low levels, has been shown to increase probiotic types of bacteria including *Bifidobacterium*. That may partially explain why inulin has been found to help prevent, or reduce the severity of, traveller's diarrhea. But that's not all; there's evidence that inulin can positively impact many aspects of our health. For example, inulin can help with calcium absorption and thus help increase bone mineral density, which is important for preventing bone loss in our later years. When combined with fructo-oligosaccharides, this prebiotic has also been shown to reduce markers of inflammation associated with inflammatory bowel disease like Crohn's and ulcerative colitis. This may be because of inulin's positive influence on *Bifidobacterium* levels as well as on butyrate production (including *Faecalibacterium prausnitzii* (page 23) a well-known butyrate-producing bacterium). Inulin tends to make us humans gassy, so it's best in moderation.

## ISOMALTO-OLIGOSACCHARIDES

Isomalto-oligosaccharides (IMO) are found in honey, and especially in sourdough bread and even gluten-free sourdough sorghum loaves. Research on animals suggests that IMO can have positive effects on the gut microbiome. In one study, by feeding mice a high-fat diet with a combination of IMO and green tea extract, scientists were able to reduce the inflammatory activity and "leaky gut" associated with a high-fat diet while improving many markers for health. Another study, this time in rats, showed that supplementing the diet with IMO resulted in a higher abundance of *Lactobacillus* (page 23). It also increased gut microbial diversity, a key indicator of balance and stability in the gut microbiome.

## LIGNINS

Plant lignins are found in flax, rye and some vegetables. One study on women found that a diet containing lignins is associated with greater gut microbial diversity. In particular, several studies show that lignins can encourage the abundance of specific bacteria with probiotic properties that enhance digestion function and mood, like *Lactobacillus rhamnosus*, *Bifidobacterium breve* and *Bifidobacterium adolescentis*.

## PECTINS

Pectins are dietary fibres with gelling properties. They are found in plants and can't be broken down by the human digestive tract. Instead, they make it to the colon, where they are fermented (transformed) by our gut bacteria into short-chain fatty acids. Pectins are known to nourish several types of gut bacteria involved in these functions, like probiotic microbes, including *Bifidobacterium* and *Lactobacillus*, and those that produce the short-chain fatty acid butyrate (page 20), notably *Faecalibacterium prausnitzii* and *Roseburia*. You'll find pectin in some of the ingredients we'll use in the recipes later, such as cranberries, kiwi fruit, apples, pears, apricots, plums and pomegranates.

## PSYLLIUM

Psyllium is a soluble, viscous fibre that soothes digestion by bulking up the stool and regulating constipation and diarrhea. It is considered by some scientists to be a "non-fermentable" fibre (one that isn't broken down by gut microbes), but recent studies indicate that it can alter the gut's ecosystem. In a study with constipated participants, adding psyllium to their diet increased levels of butyrate-producing bacteria like *Faecalibacterium* and *Roseburia*. The viscous properties of this plant husk have been shown to help regulate blood sugar and cholesterol, trapping it in the stool and carrying it out of the body.

## RESISTANT STARCHES

Resistant starches are complex plant sugars that store energy. These compounds can't be broken down by the enzymes of our digestive tract so most of them end up in the gut, where they nourish our gut microbes, which turn them into beneficial substances like butyrate (page 20). Resistant starches are divided into subcategories. Type 1 is naturally present in grains and found in foods made from wholegrain flours, like bread (especially sourdough bread, due to the long fermentation process: resistant starch is created in sourdough during the fermentation process by the LAB—lactic acid bacteria). Type 2 is also naturally present in starchy foods like green (unripe) bananas and raw potatoes. Type 3 forms in starchy foods that have been cooled or chilled, including frozen bakes, conferring prebiotic properties to these foods.

## XYLAN

Xylan is found in oat bran, wheat, corn and some fruits and vegetables, as well as milk and honey. It is a type of hemicellulose that is used to make xylo-oligosaccharides, prebiotic fibres that selectively nourish good bacteria in the gut. Xylo-oligosaccharides, like other prebiotics, have been shown to encourage growth of *Bifidobacterium* and *Lactobacillus* (pages 22–23). Because of this, it can help with inflammation and a healthy immune system function, and also increase the production of essential short-chain fatty acids that support gut health. Xylo-oligosaccharides have also been shown to improve bowel movement frequency and consistency.

# Polyphenols
## Increased levels of antioxidants

Throughout the recipes, you will see that I have incorporated ingredients high in antioxidants, especially polyphenols and flavonoids, which have been shown to nourish positive microbes. Due to their "prebiotic-like" effect, polyphenols can also positively modify gut microbiota composition. Both *in vitro* and *in vivo* studies have shown that different polyphenols can modulate the growth of specific bacterial strains. Indeed, polyphenols can increase beneficial strains, such as as *Bifidobacteria* and *Lactobacilli*, which then reduce the number of pathogens. We've incorporated polyphenols into every recipe.

## Types of polyphenols

There are more than 8,000 types of polyphenols, and it would take too long to list all the polyphenols included in the recipes in this book. There are crossovers, too, because a polyphenol can also be a prebiotic. So, I have created a chart (overleaf) with some examples of common polyphenols and the ingredients in which they can be found. Each recipe has been created to incorporate a wide range of polyphenols included in the Botanical Blends (pages 55–57) and the Fresh fruit compote (page 83).

### POLYPHENOLS CAN BE CATEGORIZED INTO FOUR MAIN GROUPS:

### FLAVONOIDS
This is the largest group and make up about 60 per cent of all polyphenols, including quercetin, kaempferol and catechins. Flavonoids may be divided into six subclasses: flavonols, flavones, flavanones, flavanols, anthocyanins, and isoflavones.

### PHENOLIC ACIDS
This group accounts for around 30 per cent of all polyphenols. Examples of phenolic acids include stilbenes and lignans, which can be found in seeds, wholegrains and fruit.

### POLYPHENOLIC AMIDES
This category includes avenanthramides, found in oats, and capsaicinoids, found in chili peppers.

### OTHER POLYPHENOLS
This group includes curcumin, found in turmeric; resveratrol, found in grapes; and ellagic acid, found in berries.

# Polyphenols throughout the book

| | CLASSIFICATION | FOUND IN |
|---|---|---|
| FLAVONOIDS | Anthocyanins | All berries (including blackberries), cherries, plums, pomegranates, and all the blue and red flower petals in the Botanical Blends (pages 55–57). |
| | Flavanols | Apples, pears, lentils, green tea, and cocoa. |
| | Flavanones | Oregano, orange peel, lemons, and all citrus fruits. |
| | Flavones | Orange, onion skins, green tea, honey, and spices. |
| | Flavonols | Marigold petals, berries, apples, pears, beans, black tea, vinegar, and vetch. |
| | Isoflavonoids | Garbanzos, soy beans, and pistachios. |
| PHENOLIC ACIDS | Hydroxybenoic acid | Strawberries, pomegranates, grapes, berries, walnuts, chocolate, and green tea. |
| | Hydroxycinnamic acid | Wheat, grains, coffee, and carrots. |
| | Lignans | Flax seeds, sesame seeds, sunflower seeds, poppy seeds, and pumpkin seeds. |
| | Stilbenes | Grapes, berries, and red wine. |

# The way you live your life

## Reducing stress: how the act of baking might help nurture the biome, mental health and mood

Stress has a negative impact on the positive microbes in the gut. Higher levels of cortisol, a common biological marker of stress, have been associated with lower levels of beneficial *Bifidobacterium*.

Baking may be a way of reducing stress, and not just by incorporating the gut-friendly ingredients we have been discussing. Being in the moment has been shown to reduce levels of the hormone cortisol. So, I want to encourage you to connect to the process of baking. It's not hard; you just need to enjoy the sense of feel and touch when you bake. Get your hands into the dough and take a quiet, contemplative moment as you sense the ingredients coming together under your fingers. Explore how this action can create an incredible change in your mood, taking you away from the stress of everyday life. (I think maybe the bottom line is that you can't pick up your mobile phone when your hands are covered in dough!)

## Exercise to increase your gut microbial diversity

Odd as it might seem to find a note on exercise in a baking book, we incorporate time outside and gentle exercise in our baking routine at the School. The routine of long, slow fermentation offers a window while you wait. Animal studies show that exercise (ranging from moderate to high in intensity) can positively influence gut microbiota diversity, which in turn could have positive effects on a range of health outcomes, including obesity, diabetes, neurological disorders and improved immunity. A study on rugby players also confirmed that they had a wider gut microbial diversity than their sedentary control group. I'm not suggesting for one second that you go out for a game of rugby mid-bake, but there is the opportunity to fit a walk into the routine.

## Connecting to your ingredients

Given that exercise has a positive impact on diversity, and we know that being in the moment lowers cortisol levels, we can combine walking and foraging for our ingredients as part of our routine. At the School, we pick wild strawberries in spring, and apples and fruit in the autumn, because there is a tremendous body of evidence for the health benefits of being outside, not least the reduction in cortisol levels. You don't have to live in the countryside to get these benefits. Simply take a stroll to the shops or, better still, to the market.

Baking can give you a break from reality and the strains of modern life. It's a very ancient form of therapy, one that can give you a feeling of connection to the food and to those you share it with. It may only be for a few minutes with a pot of tea or a cup of coffee, but taking the time to share with and nurture the people around us—our friends, family, neighbours, the people we love—can bring a sense of wellbeing. And what's really interesting is that the more you bake, and the more friendships you form, the better you feel.

# My 7 powerful ways to nourish your gut microbiome

To thrive, you need to nourish your beneficial bacteria. Modifying your diet to nourish our gut microbiome is not an exact science, but there are certain things, which are very clear from the research, that you can apply to your baking in order to enjoy a wide range of delicious bakes that support your gut health, mind and body.

These 7 principles have been applied to all the recipes in this book.

## 1. Increase fibre

One of the most powerful things you can do to support the gut is increase the amount of fibre that you eat. Fibre is key to nourishing our gut microbes (see Chapter 1, "The gut microbiome & mood").

## 2. Increase diversity

It's not enough to just increase the amount of fibre you eat. The research is clear: the wider the diversity of the food you eat, the wider the diversity of your microbes; and the wider the diversity of your microbes, the more robust your health. You can learn how to hugely increase this diversity by using my Botanical Blends on pages 55–57 in Chapter 2, "Diversity".

## 3. Ferment

The potential of fermentation to improve gut health is huge. *In vitro* studies have shown fermentation leading to increased bioavailability of key nutrients to the gut. I will cover this in more detail in Chapter 4, "The sourdough process".

## 4. Increase levels of antioxidants

Especially polyphenols and flavonoids, which have been shown to nourish positive microbes (see Chapter 1, "The gut microbiome & mood").

## 5. Increase probiotics in your bakes

Recent research points to a previously unexplored role played by gut bacteria in mental health and explores the benefits of probiotic bacteria and overall gut microbial health when it comes to stress resilience, mood, anxiety and depression. I will cover this in more detail in Chapter 3, "Probiotics" from page 38.

## 6. Reduce refined sugar

Consumption of refined sugar is linked to inflammation.

## 7. Make lifestyle changes that support the body as a whole

Make changes that affect the balance of the positive microbes in the gut and explore how the routine of making and baking sourdough can support this (see Chapter 4, "The sourdough process").

# Notes

# Diversity

In this chapter we'll cover:
Why it's not just about increasing
the amount of fibre you eat.
Why increasing the diversity of fibre
is just as important.
Botanical blends designed to feed
the good bacteria in your gut.

# Understanding what flour really is

The first thing to understand is that you must stop thinking of your ingredient as simply flour. Your bake starts in a field, in the earth; it starts with wind, rain and sun. You are baking with the ground seeds of plants that sway as the breeze catches them. Stand in a wheat field in June and you will feel the warmth of the sun's rays on a ripening harvest. Watch the butterflies chasing each other over the heads of wheat and listen to the sounds. *This* is your ingredient. This is the key.

You are baking with a plant that was planted by a farmer. The nourishment that the flour brings to your bread is based in the soil in which that plant was grown. The levels of protein and the balance of the gluten are directly related to the way in which it was grown, when it was planted and how much sunshine the plant got. So, the very first things to teach a baker are that flour is made from the seeds of a plant, that where and how it was grown matters, and that when you mill it and add it to water in your dough, it behaves as an emerging plant. All the component parts of the seed, which is perfectly designed to grow in the warmth of moist, nourishing, mineral-rich soil, are triggered. If you, the baker, can understand the intention of the plant, then you will understand the process. Fermenting baked goods and understanding the innate intention of the wheat will naturally make you a more intuitive baker.

# How do grains benefit the microbes that affect mood?

Grains are powerful prebiotics (see page 19). There are dozens of papers on the nutritional benefits of grains, but I am specifically interested in how grains might support the positive gut bacteria that impact on our mood and wellbeing.

Below is a summary of the most up-to-date evidence of the key grains used in baking and how they potentially nourish the psychobiotics (see page 62) and modulate the microbes in the gut to affect mood. It is important to understand that the most abundant phenolic compounds found in wheat are phenolic acids and flavonoids, which are located in the outer layer of the grain. This is the key research on the prebiotic power of the grains in our Botanical blends (see pages 55–57)

BASE BLEND 2 (page 55) is our base meadow blend. Spelt is our main choice of wheat in this blend. We keep Blend No. 2 at the School at all times to use as a base for all the other blends. It's a heritage blend, and while you can play with the ratios to a certain degree, I recommend that you keep the spelt at 65 per cent. This blend delivers high levels of fibre and phytonutrients. Many of our students report that they can digest heritage grains more easily. This might well be because the structure of the gluten is different and so they do not get an immune response. However, there are higher levels of fructans, which are known to aggravate irritable bowel syndrome (IBS) symptoms, so I advise a slightly longer fermentation of this blend for anyone with IBS. To ensure optimal fermentation, pop your dough in the fridge for 4–8 hours after you have left it out overnight, then bake as usual.

## WHEAT

These wild grasses enabled our species to transition from a hunter-gatherer existence to an agricultural society. They have graced our tables (and ovens) for millennia, providing a stable food source rich in fibre, slow-digesting sugars and trace elements that are essential to gut microbial health. The benefits of a diet rich in wholegrains are vast. They protect us from low-grade inflammation, which is linked to many chronic diseases of our time and also affects mental wellbeing. Wholegrains also aid vital activities by gut microbes like the production of SCFAs (short-chain fatty acids, see page 20), which support a range of activities essential for gut health and overall wellbeing.

## BARLEY

This traditional grain was one of the first to be domesticated and has been grown for 10,000 years. Barley is a source of micronutrients, vitamins B1 and B3, dietary fibre and trace elements, such as manganese, selenium, copper, chromium and phosphorus. Fibre makes up about 17 per cent of this grain's overall macronutrient profile and it is especially rich in beta-glucan. This prebiotic substance nourishes gut microbes, encouraging the presence of good bacteria like *Bifidobacterium* and *Lactobacillus plantarum*. It also stimulates the production of short-chain fatty acids.

## BUCKWHEAT

This autumnal ingredient has a nutty taste profile that makes it an exceptional flavor pairing with both sweet and savoury foods. Although commonly believed to be a grain, buckwheat is actually the seed of a flower related to rhubarb. Buckwheat contains polyphenols, including flavonols, flavonoids and chlorogenic acid, which helps with cognitive function and brain health. It is high in fibre, which makes up about 10 per cent of its macronutrient profile. Buckwheat flour is also an excellent source of plant-based, non-gluten protein, which makes up about 19 per cent of its mass in flour. These hard-to-digest compounds have prebiotic properties, such as resistant starch, polysaccharides and polyphenols, which are known to support gut microbial health. Buckwheat is also a good source of vitamins B3 (niacin), B9 (folate), K and E, and it has higher levels of copper, manganese and zinc than common grains. Its amino acid profile is also superior to that of common grains (but lower than other sources of plant protein), and it contains tryptophan, an essential component for making serotonin, "the happy hormone" (page 19).

### RYE

This cereal thrives in harsh, Northern soils, from which it gains a distinctive rich flavor and warm aroma. Compared to other cereals, rye is a good source of vitamins B3 (niacin), B9 (folate), K and E. One study showed that sourdough fermentation of (whole) rye bread triggers a better insulin response than that of refined wheat flours. This grain has a lot of dietary fibre (up to 14.6 per cent of its mass) and is a source of fructo-oligosaccharides (page 26) and arabinoxylan (page 25), prebiotic fibres that benefit the gut microbiome. In fact, studies on Scandinavians consuming rye bread indicate that it can increase levels of *Firmicutes* bacteria, which are particularly good at breaking down dietary fibre, and an increase in butyrate production, an anti-inflammatory short-chain fatty acid that supports the integrity of the gut lining (page 20). Furthermore, wholegrain rye has also been shown to improve bowel function, including transit time and frequency, lowering the risk of colon cancer.

### OATS

This cereal has high amounts of beta-glucan (page 25), a dietary fibre that is mostly broken down by gut microbes into short-chain fatty acids like propionate. Scientists think that this is part of the reason that wholegrains such as oats are able to improve cholesterol levels. Beta-glucan may also help to lower the pH in the gut, making it a better environment for good microbes and deterring potential pathogens. *In vitro* studies show that thick oat flakes (as opposed to thin ones) can encourage colonies of probiotic *Bifidobacterium* that support the activity of microbes that make butyrate (page 20). Oats are also a source of fructo-oligosaccharides (page 26), prebiotic fibres that nourish gut microbes. Studies have revealed that they can help with weight management, blood glucose control, immune system regulation and cholesterol levels.

### FLAXSEED

Flaxseed is one of the few foods I am comfortable calling a superfood. The oil in the seeds is rich in omega-3, digestible proteins, and it is one of the richest sources of alpha-linolenic acid oil and lignans. It is also a source of high-quality protein and soluble fibre and has considerable levels of phenolic compounds. Research has shown that flaxseed may possess chemo-protective properties in both animal and human studies. I'd love to say it has been studied in depth, but studies on the effect on the microbes in the gut are currently few and far between. The studies I have found to date on modulating and increasing positive bacteria in the gut are on mice, ducks, and pigs. One randomized controlled trial for humans for obese postmenopausal women in 2014 showed that flaxseed increased the proportions of beneficial *Akkermansia* and *Bifidobacterium*. It was an observation and wasn't the main focus of the study, and the authors concluded that the changes in the microbiome were unrelated to the increased insulin sensitivity that they observed in the participants. It's funny reading their conclusions in retrospect, as Tim Spector's work has specifically identified that our bacteria are key to the way we process our food and blood sugar response. So I am including flaxseed as the only ingredient without much evidence behind it, because I am convinced that, as we are in the early days of really understanding the gut microbes and the effects of specific foods, I feel it is just a matter of time before the science catches up with my gut instinct.

## Fibre and diversity are key to gut health

When I first began researching why so many people said they felt better when they baked handmade loaves, it soon became apparent that many of the people who were coming to the School were lacking the basic minimum amount of fibre per day needed to maintain a healthy gut microbiome. Gut health is more than just the *amount* of fibre, however. One of the key things emerging from the research is that the wider the diversity of the gut microbiome, and the more abundant the beneficial bacteria, the more robust your health. It is also important, though, that your gut microbial population is balanced. This correlation between gut microbe diversity and good health has been established by some of the world's leading specialists, including Tim Spector, Head of Genetic Epidemiology at King's College, London.

## It's time to rethink flour

Yes, flour is milled from grain. Mostly this grain is common wheat (*Triticum aestivum*), also known as bread wheat, a cultivated wheat species. This means bakers mostly make single-grain bakes. Even sourdough bakers will bake rye bread, spelt buns, einkorn or emmer loaves or oat cakes. But these are still bakes made from a single species. If you are lucky, you might find a seeded or mixed grain loaf, but most baking is done with just wheat.

The reverence with which bakers hold up single origin grains as the Holy Grail of artisan baking is ironic. Bakers, who are often pushing back against intensive agricultural practices, are baking with a single species of grain milled into flour. Even bakers who are using local, stone-ground, milled organic flour are actually unwittingly following the blinkered, monocultural approach of intensive agriculture.

This is a worldwide established monocultural groove that we bakers are not obliged to follow. The system we work in is diametrically opposed to our understanding of the basic requirement for a healthy gut microbiome: the need for diversity. It is time to rethink flour. It is time to apply the findings of the research on what makes a healthy gut to our most basic of foods.

It is time to change.

It is time to reclaim diversity.

It is time to stop being dictated to by an outdated industrialized system that we know is a contributing factor to reducing our gut microbial diversity and our health.

# Understanding the system

The way different countries measure their flour protein levels varies. So, if you are using Italian flour, British flour or French flour, the machines that are used to measure the protein are slightly different to those used for American flour, because they are looking for different markers. Even the gluten structure of the same grain can be different from country to country, depending on the levels of nutrients in the soil, rainfall and sunshine during the year. So again, this is a guide to flour.

I cannot emphasise enough that you will have to become familiar with your flour to be a good baker. Repetition and familiarity are the keys to success.

## Using modern varieties of grain

There are occasions when I use modern varieties, especially with recipes that need a lot of gluten, but I don't use any (if I can help it) for anyone with digestive issues. Blend Number 1 (see page 55) is a hybrid blend, a combination of modern and ancient varieties. It brings together the best properties of flavor, nutrition, and gluten structure for a small number of bakes that really need this structure, such as laminated dough.

However, if you have any doubts whatsoever when it comes to health, wellness or digestive issues, it is better to avoid modern wheat varieties. One of the problems with the way we look at flour is that we have become used to cheap, white, extensible flour, but the truth is that you can't have it both ways. If you want to bake the most nutritious, naturally flavorsome, nourishing bakes, it is best to avoid the potentially inflammatory structure of high-protein flour. This is the kind of flour that makes panettone and other breads with very open crumb structures. It often has a modern gluten structure, with high protein. This means the flour has high levels of gluten and there is more of the specific protein gliadin, which gives that open, stretchy structure whilst maintaining dough rheology (see page 187).

It's important to understand that there is no right or wrong, no absolutes, and that avoiding modern varieties completely is a complicated and very contentious area. I believe, though, that there are several factors that it is important to consider:

### DIGESTIVE ISSUES
Over the years, we've had many students at the School who have reported problems digesting high-protein, under-fermented bread, or yeasted bread, and for many people we realized that a combination of avoiding modern grains and using slow-fermented heritage grains meant they were able to enjoy baked goods again. This is not the case for everyone, though, so we approach each bake individually. For people who suffer from IBS, white flour reduces the fibre content of a blend, so we sometimes add it to freshly milled flour.

Research keeps bringing us back to discussions about the role of gliadins, the proteins most commonly associated with digestive issues. They are more prevalent in modern wheat and wheat grown conventionally. I have many unanswered questions about the gliadins in modern wheat (especially when it comes to non-coeliac gluten sensitivity), but I tend to favor ancient varieties because my students report that these grains are easier to digest, providing they are fully fermented. The mechanism for this is far from clear: each person is unique, and each variety of grain is different. Digestive issues for some may have nothing to do with the gliadins, and it may simply be that the higher natural enzymes in the grain increase fermentation, meaning the gluten or FODMAPs (Fermentable Oligosaccharides, Disaccharides, Monosaccharides and Polyols) are more broken down. Or it might be that heritage grains have a different gluten structure. I don't think there is a simple answer, because it could be a combination of factors.

### RESERVATIONS ABOUT MODERN GRAINS
I do have reservations about using modern grains, both because of the monocultural way in which they are grown, and because of the way they have been bred for a different gluten structure. This has led me to seriously question using modern grains; not just wheat, but also rye, barley and oats. More specifically, I have concerns about the levels of key nutrients and specific beneficial fibres that have been lost or reduced during development and breeding. That said, modern grains and white, roller-milled flour are needed to create structure in some bakes, and some breeders are working to breed nutrients back into modern grain. So, again, there are unanswered questions. For now, I do use modern grains when appropriate, but I reduce the amount I use whenever possible—and I blend.

### THE QUESTION OF SUSTAINABILITY
We should also consider the absolute reliance on agrichemicals, such as fertilizers, fungicides, pesticides, and herbicides, in the conventional farming practices that produce modern wheat. So, when I do use modern wheat, I use organically sourced grains, and push the fermentation process to ensure as much breakdown as possible, reducing the gluten load.

Ultimately, I know that the ancient varieties are more easily tolerated by most people, have more flavor and, in general, have a far superior nutritional profile.

# Why do you specify in your formulas how a flour is milled?
I specify how the flour is milled because the milling is a factor that affects the rate of fermentation. White roller-milled flour has more surface area, so it absorbs water faster. Stoneground flour has more enzymic activity, nutrients and bran. Milling also affects the rate of assimilation of carbohydrates, which can then affect blood sugar balance.

### HOW DO I KNOW IF A FLOUR IS ROLLER-MILLED OR STONEGROUND?
No bag of flour will ever say "roller-milled" on the label. It's just the standard way that almost all conventional flour is milled, so you can assume that unless the label says "stoneground", the flour will have been roller-milled.

# White flour

There are lots of different kinds of white flour and we use them here for different purposes.

### WHITE, ROLLER-MILLED BREAD FLOUR

At 12–14 per cent protein, this is the standard type of bread flour found in most supermarkets. It is pretty much devoid of nutrients, apart from whatever pharmacological fortification has been added back in according to the mandatory requirements of some countries. Nevertheless, this is still a flour we use at the School. It provides structure and we use it as a base flour to blend with. We also use this flour to refresh our starters, but never on its own to bake bread, because alone, white roller-milled flour simply doesn't have enough nutritional density.

### WHITE ROLLER-MILLED FLOUR (FOR CAKES AND PASTRIES)

Again, this flour is normally found in supermarkets, and has 10–11 per cent protein. It is generally more challenging to find an organic version. We don't use much of this day to day at the School. Instead we use a finely milled and sieved wholegrain Botanical blend. Occasionally, white roller-milled flour is useful to reduce the fibre load, which can be helpful if someone has IBS.

### WHITE, STONEGROUND FLOUR

This is a flour that is gaining in popularity and can be found at specialist baking suppliers online. Alternatively, you can go to a local mill and meet the miller, or you can mill and sift your own. You could even just sift a bag of stoneground wholegrain flour.

### WHITE SPELT

This is a much more specialist flour and perhaps one of my favourite flours to bake with. It creates an open crumb and has a sweet, light, nutty flavor. It is also more challenging as a bread flour and needs "propping up" with high-protein bread flour to make a boule (see my previous book, *The Sourdough School*).

### WHITE RYE

This is another specialist flour, but one that is worth adding to your repertoire. It is lighter than wholegrain rye, and so can be used more subtly, to add depth of flavor without compromising on texture.

# Wholegrain flour

Wheat has been at the heart of civilisation since the dawn of agriculture, and wholegrain is at the heart of what we teach at the School. It combines astounding elastic properties (gluten), dietary fibre and prebiotics, flavor, and a whole host of health benefits for the body and our gut microbes. There are specific fibres such as arabinoxylan (page 25), resistant starch (page 27) and wheat dextrin (page 25) that help modulate gut bacteria and increase production of the short-chain fatty acids acetate, propionate, and butyrate (page 20). Like buckwheat and rye, this cereal provides good levels of vitamins B3 (niacin), B5 (pantothenic acid), B9 (folate), E and K, as well as manganese, copper and magnesium. There are many other bioactive components in wheat, including polyphenols, which have antioxidant and anti-tumour properties, and also improve cardiovascular function. Studies also show that whole wheat can help lower body weight and reduce low-grade inflammatory markers in the body that are associated with chronic illnesses, including depression.

Specifying simply "wholegrain" is a bit like specifying just "fruit". What kind? Apples? Pears? Bananas? Apricots? Blackberries? Wholegrain flour is the fruit of the grasses. Each type is different, and to expect all wholegrain flour to behave and taste the same is as silly as expecting every kind of fruit to be just like an apple. Above, right are some simple guidelines to finding the kind of wholegrain flour we use at the School.

## WE MAINLY USE STONEGROUND, FRESH-MILLED WHOLEGRAIN FLOUR

It is almost always organic, or equivalent. We often use spelt, einkorn and emmer wholegrain. All the recipes that specify wholegrain will work with these flours.

## DON'T WORRY IF YOU CAN'T FIND IT

I appreciate that organic, stoneground wholegrain flour isn't always available. So, don't get frustrated. It is your kitchen and you are feeding your family. All the recipes throughout this book will work with a modern wholegrain roller-milled flour. You might find that they ferment at a slightly different rate, because modern wheat has a different structure. In the main, they will just take a little longer to ferment, so you will need to adjust your timings accordingly.

# Stepping out of the system: wholegrain flours and home milling

## The start of monoculture

One of the most respected people in the world of heritage grain is archaeobotanist John Letts, who teaches the heritage grain module at the Sourdough School. When I met John, he was growing hundreds of different grains. His eyes lit up as he showed me grains spanning 100,000 years. He told me how the Victorians wanted to select the "best" single strains of wheat and breed them into landraces that suited specific conditions in the fields at that moment in time, often selecting from a field with 400–500 varieties, and taking it down to just one. This was the start of monoculture.

## How the system destroyed natural diversity

As we systemized food production, we lost flavor, genetic diversity, and so much of nature's answer to climate change: the ability of a crop to adapt to changing weather patterns. Lack of genetic diversity in grains is now one of the single biggest threats to global food security. We also lost something hugely significant: the diversity in the grains. In other words, we lost the range of prebiotics needed to maintain a diverse gut microbiota. Each and every kind of grain delivered different kinds of fibre and had nutritional value. As we intensified agricultural practices using herbicides, we lost even more. We lost wild mustard seeds, hedgerow fruits, wild oats, herbs and edible flowers, and varieties of barley, durum wheat and rye.

## Finding what was lost

The answer came on a summer's day in northern Italy. I was visiting a mill with which I had been working for many years, and met an amazing Italian baker called Gabrielle Bonci. He is famous for his pizza, but his incredible passion for bread was what I loved about him. He is the epitome of generosity, and he shared not just his knowledge, but also his hospitality and warmth, introducing me to farmers with whom he had worked for a lifetime. He took me to meet a family who have grown and milled their own wheat (one with lots of varieties in the field) for generations. The valley in which the grain was grown was one of the most beautiful places I have ever stood. It was magical, with the warm June sun ripening a field of diverse grains dancing in the breeze. The blend in the fields had been bolstered with varieties collected from the Seed Bank at Aleppo just as the war threatened this incredible seed conservation centre. The blend was called *Mazi*, meaning "together".

Butterflies and bees were collecting nectar. The crop was so elegant. The grains were black and green and golden; they were copper, mahogany and iridescent. I remember picking a bouquet and looking across the valley at the olive groves and feeling a strong sense of connection. But it was about more than just the grain. There were cornflowers and wild oregano at my feet, and there were roses in the hedgerows that would bring rosehips in September. There were blackberries and wild oats and peas in the margins. I saw it all, and it was as though time stood still as the real meaning of diversity was right there in front of me. It has been there all the time and yet we hadn't seen it.

We have all been blindly baking according to the monocultural, intensive agricultural methods that have been the very cause of the loss of diversity. Even the most radical sourdough bakers, who pride themselves on baking against the mass-produced system, are unknowingly following that very system in the way they approach their baking.

Can you imagine a Neolithic hunter-gatherer wandering around looking for spelt grain for a long, slow-fermented spelt loaf? It's ludicrous. They would have simply used what was available: anything edible. We devolved as we systemized our most basic food, both physically and mentally.

# Rebel: make connections and find other bakers

### BAKERS HOLD THE BALANCE OF POWER

The system is not indestructible. There is still time to find a way to reverse it. We can stop the systematic destruction of natural diversity, nourish our gut microbiome and protect the planet. This is a call to arms—and you can start today. We choose our ingredients. We mix and make what we bake and eat. As bakers, we hold the power.

### WE ARE A COMMUNITY

Small, anarchistic connections run deep. We must share and draw together. Part of the change is about finding other bakers. When you meet another baker, one who inspires you, you have strengthened the link. You will find meetings, forums and events where grain lovers gather, and you can both share and gain a huge amount of knowledge. Social media is another good place to connect.

### FIND AND SUPPORT YOUR LOCAL FARMER

Find a farmer who wants to grow and create population wheat, and a miller who wants to mill it. Then support them, because it isn't easy. If you run a bakery and you can commit to using the grain that a farmer grows, you will seriously reduce the amount of financial risk taken by the farmer. It will help him to support you, and vice versa.

### THINK GLOBALLY: WE ARE ONE PLANET

Expand your horizons and increase your options. Growing population grains or ancient varieties takes time and understanding and requires making a change from the conventional system. This takes resources that many farmers don't have. It is hard and often only the bravest farmers have the strength of mind and financial ability to make these changes. Even if these farmers are not on your doorstep, you can still support them.

### ONE PLANET, ONE BIOSPHERE

While I encourage every baker to go and find their local farmer, I also feel that we are one. We are one planet. One biosphere. Together we are whole, and once I made the connection between the soil, our food and our own microbial communities, my aim has been to nurture that connection. So above all, my principles are rooted firmly in organic systems over and above all other considerations.

# Why we mill our own blends

**Milling your own blends is the antithesis of commercial baking. You can hand-select each ingredient according to the season. It is an art.**

### DIVERSITY

Perhaps the most important reason to mill your own flour is that you get to create diversity blends that instantly increase the diversity factor of your loaves. We add in other ingredients that are not grains, such as herbs, beans, spices and flowers.

### PERFUME

Freshly ground flour smells exquisite. It is warm as it comes out of the mill and the aroma of freshly milled wheat is like a hay barn on a summer's day. I get especially excited about barley: if you could smell golden sunshine, it would smell like freshly milled barley. I try to use barley in all my bakes.

### FREEDOM

Your flavor palate will explode. If you are creative, you will take this concept and make it your own. When I create a bake, I want access to a full range of flavor, color, texture, and nutrients, and blending is a brilliant way to do this.

### TEXTURE

Milling your own flour puts you in in full control of texture. This is especially fun because you can kibble (roughly mill your grain). Changing the texture of your flour and creating kibble has other benefits, such as helping to moderate blood sugar response.

### NUTRITION

Fresh flour is more nutritious because it hasn't had time to oxidize. As flour matures, it oxidizes which can be helpful, because this facilitates protein development which is needed for breadmaking but not for cake making.

# Nourishing your gut from the offset

You can connect closely to what you are baking with. You can play. You can experiment with flavor combinations. In the end, all good bakes are about texture and flavor, and milling your own flour means you can control both.

At the School, we make our own blends to maximize the different types of fibre in the flour. This feeds the widest range of beneficial microbes throughout all our bakes.

Blending is the most powerful base you can give to your bakes. It creates instant diversity. From the moment you mix your bake, you have already included a wide range of known prebiotic fibre. This means you are nourishing your gut flora from the very first bite.

# Can I use ordinary wholegrain flour from the supermarket for these recipes?

Yes. You can simply go to the supermarket, buy some wholegrain flour and bake the recipes in this book. It's easy and convenient, and I appreciate that, for many people, milling your own flour might be too time-consuming. Time is short and this is real life. If you are short of time, try at the very least to find different varieties of organic, stoneground flour and mix them up.

**HOW TO BLEND IF YOU DO NOT HAVE A MILL**
You may be more restricted, and the blends you will be able to create might be less diverse than the blends outlined on pages 55–57, but it is still possible to create diversity. I suggest starting with a mix of heritage flours, such as 700g spelt, 100g emmer and 100g einkorn. Then add 50g fine polenta and 50g rye flour—that alone will give you a diversity score (see page 55) of 5. You can also add a tablespoon of cocoa or dried herbs appropriate to the flavor you want to create. For example, dried mint would work well in a flour for the chocolate brownie cake on page 156.

# The Sourdough School Botanical blends

## Diversity is nourishing

We evolved with natural diversity and followed the seasons. For early Neolithic hunter-gatherers, collecting a wide range of food to incorporate into their daily diet was an unconditional gift given by nature.

Our great-grandfathers set about industrialising our food, systematically selecting specific grains, which they named and narrowed down. Without realizing it, they destroyed and discarded the thing we need most: diversity.

The research is irrefutable; diversity is one of the key factors affecting gut health. But achieving diversity in the current system is very complicated. The farmers and the millers are trapped within this system. But we can break out.

The answer is to rethink flour and recreate this diversity by creating our own botanical blends. This simple act is a powerful and absolute rejection of monoculture.

My botanical blends were inspired by standing in fields of grain and seeing a beautiful sea of color and diversity. These blends reflect the way that these grains grew naturally, before agriculture. There are wild oats, brome grasses, cornflowers, poppies, fragrant herbs, such as oregano, and wild legumes, such as vetch and charlock (wild mustard seeds, known as "Poor Man's Pepper"). Each plant has different biomolecules and this diversity is exactly what our own gut microbes need to thrive.

The blends below are a guide. They are not prescriptive or fixed in any way, but generally I try to use 80 per cent grain and 20 per cent non-grain diverse ingredients.

Think about the season, and your location, and make these factors the base for creating your own blends. Although I've created these blends, the anarchist in me will be celebrating when you start making your own blends with your own seasonal, local ingredients.

**MAKE IT YOUR OWN**
We use our blends for both leaven and for the wholegrain flour in the formulas. You can mix and match them. If you don't have all the ingredients, then play a little but try to keep the ratios of grain: non-grain additions the same.

**STORING YOUR BLENDS**
Make up your favorite blends in a jar (you can freeze the grains to kill any bugs before mixing your blend). I make up my blends about every three months to keep the herbs and spices fresh. I only mill flour as I need it, because the flour blends are exquisitely soft and fragrant as they are milled. The antioxidants are higher this way, too, as they have not had time to oxidize. You will always lose a bit of flour in the mill, so add in an extra 5g.

**DIVERSITY SCORE** Every recipe in this book has a diversity score. Increasing the diversity of ingredients we consume in turn increases the diversity in our gut microbiome. The diversity score for each recipe is calculated according to the number of diverse ingredients it contains. (With sugar, only sugars like coconut sugar or maple syrup are counted as diverse ingredients. Likewise, with salt, only using sea salt or rock salt will add to diversity.) Research suggests that we should be aiming to consume a diversity of 30 different ingredients each week. I think we can do better than that. When I started creating the Botanical Blends and the other bakes in this book, my aim was to get close to a score of 30 with just one bite.

**MILLING TIP** Whatever mill you are using, my top tip is to use a fine sieve to sieve your flour, and re-mill the larger particles to achieve a fine flour.

You can use either fresh or dried herbs and flowers in these blends, but bear in mind that if using fresh, the flavor will be less concentrated. I often use fresh rose petals, fresh lilac flowers, violets, and the tops of nettles.

# Base blend no. 1
# Hybrid
## both modern & ancient

There are some bakes that need a modern gluten structure, such as the advanced bakes (pages 168–82). They simply do not work without some gluten strength. For those who do not have any digestive issues with modern grains, this blend has the best of both wholegrain and heritage, freshly milled flour, and the crumb structure offered by modern varieties. This blend is lower in fibre than our other blends, so it has an important role for anyone with IBS who cannot digest large amounts of fibre. MAKES 1KG

**DIVERSITY SCORE** 1 [if you do not have a mill]

200g any organic, stoneground, wholegrain flour
800g organic, white flour, 12–13.5 per cent protein

If you don't have a mill, sieve the flours together and use immediately.

**DIVERSITY SCORE** 21+ [if you have a mill]

200g your choice of freshly milled Blends no. 3–6
800g organic, white flour, 12–13.5 per cent protein

If you are using a mill, follow the milling procedure according to the mill manufacturer's instructions.

# Base blend no. 2
# Meadow

This is our signature blend at the School.

MAKES ABOUT 1KG   **DIVERSITY SCORE** 12

650g spelt
80g einkorn wheat
80g emmer wheat
40g barley
20g naked oats
50g rye
20g poppy seeds
20g buckwheat
20g flax seeds
15g dried peas
5g dried edible meadow flowers of your choice, such as cornflower, mallow flower or oregano flowers
A small handful of dried nettles

Simply follow the milling procedure according to the manufacturer's instructions.

# High-antioxidant blends

## Blend no. 3
## Red
### polyphenols

MAKES ABOUT 1KG **DIVERSITY SCORE** 22

800g Blend no. 2 (page 55)
50g red quinoa
100g dried red or purple corn
2 papery outer layers red onion skin
20 dried red kidney beans
1 tablespoon pink peppercorns
2 large pinches of dried red rose petals
8 dried rosehips
3 tablespoons dried hibiscus flowers
2 tablespoons dried dulse
1–2 small dried red chili peppers, broken up (optional)

Follow the mill manufacturer's instructions for milling.

## Blend no. 4
## Blue
### anthocyanidins

MAKES ABOUT 1KG **DIVERSITY SCORE** 22

700g Blend no. 2 (page 55)
200g blue barley or black emmer wheat
100g dried blue corn
20 cornflower heads
8g fennel seeds, toasted just before milling
2 tablespoons black tea
30g cocoa beans
7 black peppercorns
10g mustard seeds
1 tablespoon dried lavender (Lavandula angustifolia),
    such as Hidcote or Munstead
30 butterfly pea flower or mallow flower heads (optional—
    not always easy to buy locally or organically, but if you can
    get them, they'll add color and boost the polyphenols)

Follow the mill manufacturer's instructions for milling.

## Blend no. 5
## Golden
### carotenoids

MAKES ABOUT 1KG **DIVERSITY SCORE** 23

800g Blend no. 2 (see page 55)
100g dried golden corn
80g barley
2 tablespoons bee pollen
10 dried marigold flowers (Calendula)
3 tablespoons chamomile flowers
10g golden mustard seeds
20g toasted golden flax seeds, toasted just before milling
20g dried yellow or orange lentils
10g ground turmeric (optional)
8 white peppercorns
2 papery outer layers yellow onion skin

Follow the mill manufacturer's instructions for milling.

## Blend no. 6
## Green
### flavonoids

MAKES ABOUT 1KG **DIVERSITY SCORE** 21

900g Blend no. 2 (page 55)
20g green tea
30 dried green peas
10 dried mung beans
1 tablespoon green peppercorns
2 tablespoons dried green seaweed
1 dried bay leaf
10–15 dried oregano flowers, with leaves
10 dried nettle leaves
small handful of dried lemon verbena

Follow the mill manufacturer's instructions for milling.

# Blend no. 7
# Spiced

MAKES ABOUT 1KG **DIVERSITY SCORE** 23

700g Blend no. 2 (page 55)
80g rye
80g khorasan wheat
20g cocoa nibs
2.5cm (1-inch) piece of cinnamon stick
10g coriander seeds, toasted just before milling
15 dried black beans
4 cloves
4 dried allspice berries
1 tablespoon wheatgerm, toasted just before milling
grating of fresh nutmeg
½ teaspoon ground ginger (optional)

Follow the mill manufacturer's instructions for milling.

# Blend no. 8
# Oriental
## flavones

MAKES ABOUT 1KG **DIVERSITY SCORE** 20

700g Blend no. 2 (page 55)
150g khorasan wheat
30g sesame seeds, toasted just before milling
60g black rice
dried peel of 2 limes
8 sanshō peppercorns (these have a lovely lime flavor;
    if you can't get them, use green peppercorns)
large pinch of dried cherry blossom (optional)
2 tablespoons dried wakame seaweed
4 cloves

Follow the mill manufacturer's instructions for milling.

# Blend no. 9
# Eastern
## flavones

MAKES ABOUT 1KG **DIVERSITY SCORE** 18

700g Blend no. 2
300g khorasan wheat
dried peel of 2 oranges
2 large pinches of dried rose petals
5 cardamom pods
a large pinch of saffron
a pinch of dried orange blossoms

Follow the mill manufacturer's instructions for milling.

# Blend no. 10
# Bean
## isoflavones

MAKES ABOUT 1KG **DIVERSITY SCORE** 10

700g dried garbanzos
300g dried mixed beans, including mung beans, black-
    eyed beans, black turtle beans, lima beans, haricot
    beans, pinto beans, red kidney beans, rose cocoa beans,
    and alubia beans

Follow the mill manufacturer's instructions for milling.

# Diversity muesli mixes

While the flour blends are the base for biodiversity in all our bakes, mueslis are the key to super-boosting your range and diversity score. At the School, we use these mixes in the diversity breads (our breads made using the botanical blends on pages 55–57) and in our porridges. Sometimes I make my muesli from scratch, but often I find an organic version and add the more expensive ingredients or the ones I particularly like. It's a shortcut, but it's a good one on so many levels, because you can vary your muesli regularly with no effort, you don't have to bulk buy, and it is fresher when bought in smaller quantities.

Oats are at the heart of muesli, and they're one of the most important ingredients at the School. Oats are humble and affordable, and have high amounts of beta-glucan (see page 25).

I often add my own dried cherries and mulberries to muesli mixes. I also add vanilla powder, chopped bittersweet chocolate, and pistachios. I like what I like, but make it yours. Here is a guide to some of the things I look for in a diverse muesli mix. Aim for at least 20 ingredients, with more if you can. My mixes generally have a combination of 30 ingredients, giving a 30 on the diversity score!

> A word of caution to anyone suffering from IBS—you may need to experiment to find a mix that suits you. Avoid adding dried fruits and seeds.

## Making your own muesli mix

**Make up any combination you like, following the proportions given here.**

**60 PER CENT FLAKES**
A mix of oats, rye flakes, spelt flakes, barley flakes, wheat flakes, puffed quinoa, puffed rice, buckwheat flakes, coconut flakes.

**10 PER CENT DRIED FRUIT**
Including raisins, golden raisins, apricots, blueberries, dates, banana chips, cranberries, goji berries, dried plums, cherries, figs.

**5–10 PER CENT FREEZE-DRIED FRUIT**
A little goes a long way. Include blackcurrants, raspberries, cranberries. You could also add some freeze-dried beet.

**10 PER CENT NUTS**
Activated nuts (which have been soaked in water and salt and then dehydrated) are better. Include nuts such as hazelnuts, almonds, Brazil nuts, cashews, macadamia nuts, pistachios, pine nuts.

**10 PER CENT SEEDS**
Seeds are delicious and highly nutritious. Try golden flax seeds, pumpkin seeds, sunflower seeds, poppy seeds, fennel seeds, sesame seeds.

**3 PER CENT SPICES**
Try adding spices such as cinnamon, dried ginger, mixed spice, vanilla powder, or nutmeg.

# Notes

# Eating symbiotically

So far, we have looked at the relationship between the gut and the brain, and established that a robust, balanced gut microbiome thrives on increased fibre intake, diversity of food and the presence of polyphenols. We have also learned that fermentation increases the bioavailability of some of the key influencers (fibre, polyphenols and minerals), but there is one more significant factor to consider: live bacteria, known as probiotics.

# What are probiotics?

**Essentially, probiotics are defined as viable microorganisms that provide health benefits by improving the microbial balance in the intestine of the host.**

Many of the same families of probiotic can be found in the sourdough process in the form of lactic acid bacteria (LAB). They do the work of transforming the structure of the flour, making it more nutritious and more digestible by breaking it down, just as they do in your gut. They are then killed, as their thermal death point is about 45–60°C (113–140°F). LAB are found across many fermented foods, including pickles, kefirs, yogurts, and vinegars. In these foods, the bacteria are actually still live.

There are some significant studies with results showing that certain strains of these LAB are so effective at modulating the mood that they could give current pharmaceutical drugs a run for their money. The term "psychobiotics" has been coined to describe this novel class of probiotics that could potentially be used to treat psychiatric diseases. It is very early days, but in preliminary studies they have been shown to have a positive effect on mood, via the microbiota–gut–brain axis (Dinan, Stanton and Cryan, 2013).

So far these psychobiotics have been most extensively studied in a psychiatric setting with patients suffering from irritable bowel syndrome (IBS). Patients reported positive effects when treated with organisms including *Bifidobacterium infantis*. Scientists are discovering that symptoms of depression and chronic fatigue syndrome may be alleviated by the anti-inflammatory actions of certain psychobiotics. (Borre et al., 2014.)

## Probiotics are part-timers

Probiotics often have a transient effect, meaning that while you are eating them, they may be found in the gut, but once you stop eating them, they can fade away. This is why incorporating them into your daily diet is an important way to support your gut and maintain health and wellbeing.

Each recipe in Chapter 5 includes either a live ingredient within the recipe, or a suggestion of a live accompaniment to serve alongside the bake. The bacteria within them are incredibly numerous. If you keep a live wild milk kefir, sourdough starter, vinegar, kombucha or indeed any wild ferment, you will have no way of knowing exactly what microbes are in there. In many ways it doesn't matter, but for many people keeping live bacteria can be time-consuming, and so you might find it easier to simply buy a live product that contains specific bacteria.

## Is it really such a radical idea for living microbes to enhance gut function?

The concept of a relationship between live bacteria and a healthy gut is not a new one. The famous Russian scientist Ilya Ilyich Mechnikov theorized that health could be enhanced, and senility delayed, by manipulating the intestinal microbiome with the host-friendly bacteria found in yogurt. He was right, and science has finally begun to catch up with his early radical observations. Today, these probiotics are not only the subject of intense global research, but they are also the source of a multi-billion dollar international industry. For the pharmaceutical industry, the fact that these microbes are transient provides them with a perfect and profitable product. Many of the food companies, who have almost unlimited resources, are already using well-researched strains in our everyday food.

Fermented crème pâtissière from the Fig & walnut slices on page 172. The recipes in Chapter 5 include probiotic accompaniments.

# Identifying specific strains

Despite it being early days, it is possible to identify exact strains. They are already being used in our everyday foods, but let me be absolutely clear in saying that we don't yet know that all these bacteria benefit us.

Although probiotics are the future of food, we actually evolved with these bacteria and they have always been there. Once you understand how fermentation works, you can try culturing specific strains and inoculating a range of substrates, such as fruit syrups, milk or cream, with strains of specific bacteria from probiotic supplements or even from kefir, yogurt and kombucha where the manufacturer has shared this information on the packaging. I often use or "borrow" strains in this way at the School.

Perhaps the easiest way to include specific bacteria in your diet is to look out for them when you are shopping. Most companies list them in the ingredients or publish research on them. Although it is still early days for research on all strains, they are still easily identifiable, and are available in yogurt (both dairy and non-dairy) and kefirs in the supermarket.

It's hard to say exactly how successful home inoculation is, and I've had different results with different species, but on the whole I have had the most success with inoculating milk and making yogurt. Personally, I feel it is far better and more powerful to inoculate with a live species already established in its substrates, such as by using an already active live yogurt. However, those wanting to play with strain-specific probiotic supplements, can choose to look into which prebiotic substrate that the particular bacteria in the supplement like and adapt their approach accordingly.

My most successful experiences of this have been when using kvass or fruit syrups, which I have used many times to create strain-specific, live, fermented beverages; but these often take 2–3 days to establish.

With dairy it is easy. I use about 500ml (18fl oz) whole organic milk to 1 capsule of probiotic supplement. Keep the milk at 34°C (93°F) overnight, and it is then ready to use. If you want to experiment, you must be sure to keep everything sterilized (see below). Store your culture in the fridge and use the yogurt within three days. Trust your instincts; your milk should now look and taste like fresh yogurt. Anything other than this should be discarded.

It can be a bit hit-and-miss, and sealed syrups need burping regularly or they will (literally) explode. At other times, nothing whatsoever will happen, which has led me to question if the bacteria in some of the supplements we are sold are even alive.

## Health and safety

I have three key pieces of advice about inoculation.
- Sterilize everything. There are plenty of ways to do so, but whichever way you choose, remember that you are growing bacteria. You really do not want to end up growing pathogens for the sake of a few minutes spent sterilizing your equipment.
- Trust your senses. If it looks or smells bad, discard it.
- Be patient and give the ferment time to establish itself. As the lactic acid bacteria start producing lactic and acetic acid, the pH will decrease (becoming more acidic). This acidity is hugely unwelcoming for almost all other microbes and creates a "members-only club", which is too hostile for pathogenic bacteria to survive. This is why fermentation has been used as a means of preserving food for millennia.

# Probiotics and live bacteria: the ones to look out for

There are hundreds of bacteria to choose from, so I have selected the significant findings on some of the key bacteria and reviewed the research on their beneficial effects on mood, health and the gut microbiome. The list below is by no means conclusive, and there is new research coming out daily. We are at the very frontier of discovering how specific strains can affect our mental health.

I cannot emphasize strongly enough that the information below is based on highly specific strains of bacteria, developed under laboratory conditions, that I cannot guarantee will be present in your ferments. However, the growing evidence showing the benefits that these families of bacteria have on our health cannot be ignored.

### BIFIDOBACTERIUM LACTIS: A KEY PLAYER

This subspecies of *Bifidobacterium*, also referred to as *Bifidobacterium animalis subsp. lactis* due to reclassification, is one of the world's most researched probiotics. It is subdivided into many strains with an overall plethora of beneficial effects for health, such as treating bloating in people with functional bowel problems like IBS, reducing antibiotic-linked diarrhea, and supporting a healthy gut microbiome by improving intestinal pH and encouraging short-chain fatty acid (SCFA) production. One study even found that, in the future, *B. lactis* may be able to help protect the gut lining of coeliac patients exposed to gliadin (the reactive protein in gluten) and help repair damage already done to the gut. Consuming yogurt with *B. lactis* in it has also been shown to have a positive impact on the emotion-forming parts of the brain.

### LACTOBACILLUS ACIDOPHILUS: A KEY PLAYER

*Lactobacillus acidophilus* is perhaps the most famous name in the probiotic domain. By producing lactic acid, *L. acidophilus* deters pathogens both in cultured dairy and in the gut, as the lactic acid helps to balance the pH. There are many applications for *L. acidophilus* in promoting health and immune function, and thus staving off illness. It can also help to reduce bloating in people with functional bowel disorders like IBS and reduce acute diarrhoea, whether it's "Delhi belly" or antibiotic-induced. It may even help treat *Clostridium difficile* (C. diff), a serious bowel infection. Recent research also shows that *L. acidophilus* can be instrumental in easing stress and anxiety and treating depression.

### LACTOBACILLUS BULGARICUS

This species of probiotic has been shown to be effective in treating acute diarrhea. Furthermore, the combination of probiotic bacteria found in yogurt, including *L. bulgaricus*, can also influence the emotion centres of the brain in healthy people via the gut–brain axis. *L. bulgaricus* has also been shown, in combination with other strains of probiotics, to inhibit the action of kyunerine in mice, a metabolite associated with depression that can cross the blood–brain barrier.

### LACTOBACILLUS FERMENTUM

This species of *Lactobacillus* is common in traditional, fermented dairy products around the world and also naturally occurs in breast milk. It has been attributed a variety of potential health benefits. In particular, women can benefit from consuming probiotic dairy with *L. fermentum* as it has been shown to stimulate important *Lactobacillus* colonies in the vagina and out-compete pathogens and yeasts that cause infections. In animals, it has been shown to significantly improve the gut microbiome. In combination with other probiotic species present in cultured dairy, *L. fermentum* can help balance the pH, deter invaders, increase SCFA production, stimulate *Lactobacillus* populations and reduce cells' oxidative stress.

## LACTOBACILLUS PARACASEI

This probiotic species of microbe can be found in the gut and in fermented foods. It has been shown to relieve the symptoms of diverticulitis, especially in combination with a high-fibre diet. Other studies indicate that it can also help with acute diarrhea and reduce symptoms of gastroenteritis. In combination with other strains of probiotic bacteria, *L. paracasei* has been shown to help induce and maintain remission in patients with ulcerative colitis. Studies in people undergoing flu vaccination showed that it may even improve immune function.

## LACTOBACILLUS PLANTARUM: A KEY PLAYER

This species of probiotic *Lactobacillus* is a very important member of my sourdough starter. It is found in many fermented foods, including sauerkraut and cocoa beans. It's one of the reasons I use my starter as an inoculant for the Sourdough fizz (page 92) and Breakfast pots (page 122) and I am honestly delighted to host this LAB. More and more research indicates that L. plantarum has a role to play in supporting good mental health. Studies show that this microbe has the ability to produce GABA (page 19), an important amino acid that can help alleviate anxiety. L. plantarum also produces serotonin (page 19), the "happy chemical" known for its ability to stabilize mood, and also involved in digestion and the body's essential motor functions.

## LACTOBACILLUS RHAMNOSUS: A KEY PLAYER

*L. rhamnosus* is a naturally occurring probiotic microbe that may play a role in various aspects of health. Several studies indicate that it can play a role in maintaining the gut barrier, regulating immune responses and intestinal motility as well as the enteric nervous system of the gut. In women, ingesting probiotics with *L. rhamnosus* can stimulate beneficial colonies of bacteria in the vagina and help deter bacterial and yeast infections. However, the most exciting possibility for *L. rhamnosus* is this species' potential for treating anxiety, mood disorders and stress. These bacteria can act via the vagus nerve (the gut–brain highway) to produce changes in GABA expression (see page 19). There is growing evidence to support its role in suppressing negative physiological responses to stress, anxiety and despair in animals, research that scientists are currently attempting to verify in humans. (Yunes et al., 2016).

## LACTOCOCCUS LACTIS CREMORIS

This subspecies of *Lactococcus* is active in kefir and buttermilk. A recent investigation of its effect on milk showed its ability to enhance the nutritional profile of the milk, providing several health-promoting effects. It can turn milk fat into conjugated linoleic acid (CLA), which has great potential for human health, with anti-cancer, anti-inflammatory, anti-obesity and anti-atherosclerotic plaque functions (among others). *L. lactis cremoris* can also increase levels of polyunsaturated fats, which can support a healthy metabolism and prevent chronic diseases.

### LACTOCOCCUS LACTIS LACTIS

This subspecies of *Lactococcus* is not only influential on the brain, but also women's health. In a study of healthy female volunteers who were given yogurt with a combination of naturally-occurring probiotics, including this one, researchers discovered that these beneficial bacteria had the ability to influence the emotion and sensation centres in the brain. Furthermore, it could be helpful in preventing vaginal infections in women when taken in conjunction with antibiotics.

### LEUCONOSTOC MESENTEROIDES

These bacteria have been found to thrive in extreme environments and are also found in fermented milk and cabbage (think kimchi and sauerkraut). They are known to produce metabolites during fermentation that contribute to the unique features and benefits of cultured dairy, such as acetate and lactate. The latter can protect the gut and lower its pH (making it more stable and less prone to invasion), while acetate is a SCFA (see page 20) that contributes to gut microbiome health.

### LEUCONOSTOC PSEUDOMESENTEROIDES

Like its relative (see left), *L. pseudomesenteroides* helps to stabilize fermented foods, fighting off pathogens and producing acidic metabolites that keep food edible, including sourdough. It's resistant to several antibiotics, which is why it's a candidate for probiotic status, as it can fight off pathogens that may invade when antibiotics disturb the microbial ecosystems of the body.

### STREPTOCOCCUS THERMOPHILUS

*S. thermophilus* has a wide range of health-promoting properties spanning digestion and immunity, mostly combined with other probiotic bacteria that naturally occur in fermented dairy. By fermenting milk, it reduces the lactose and modifies its properties, which slows its transit through the digestive tract. This is why people who are lactose-sensitive are often able to consume cultured dairy like yogurt and kefir. *S. thermophilus* has also been shown to help reduce inflammation and aid immune system reactions. In a specifically developed probiotic cocktail, a combination of microbes, including *S. thermophilus*, were able to help with Crohn's disease as well as working to prevent intestinal permeability ("leaky gut") and fighting off specific pathogens. In yogurt, *S. thermophilus* has been found to be able to influence the emotion and sensation areas of the female brain.

## How can we use this information?

Although our understanding of psychobiotics is just beginning, many of these families of microbes can already be found in everyday fermented foods that we have eaten for thousands of years. At the Sourdough School, we always aim to use yogurt, kefir and other inoculations with a minimum of five LAB strains (most of the ones we use range from 5–14+ strains), and we look for those strains that are well-documented as having health benefits wherever possible.

Probiotic rich, diversity Live sourdough donuts (page 180), nourishing your gut microbiome.

# Smoothie filling

Thick, luscious and delicious, I often serve this instead of cream alongside many of the bakes in Chapter 5.

▶ **INGREDIENTS**

25g (1 oz) chia seeds
25g (1 oz) ground flax seeds
25g (1 oz) mixed sunflower and pumpkin seeds
4 squares of chocolate
250g (9oz) kefir
½ teaspoon maca powder (optional)
1 tablespoon vanilla essence
small handful of blueberries
½ avocado

Add all the ingredients, except the blueberries and avocado, to a blender and leave to soak overnight so that the chia seeds absorb the moisture.

The next day, when ready to blend, add the blueberries and avocado and blitz. It should be very thick, like a set yogurt. Use immediately; this is delicious spread on my Diversity pikelets (see page 129).

## Variations

You could add any flavors you like, such as cardamom, orange peel, raspberries or blackberries. Try adding Brazil nuts and walnuts. You can make this with any ingredients you like; the more ingredients, the higher the diversity score!

▶ **INGREDIENTS**

1 litre (1¾ pints) whole milk (for cultured yogurt)
   or fresh cream (for cultured cream)
6 tablespoons organic, plain,
   whole-milk live yogurt
1 tablespoon milk kefir (optional)

*You will need a food thermometer*

Tip To get a thicker set, strain it through a cheesecloth-lined sieve over a bowl for a few hours before transferring to the sterilized jar.

# Yogurt and cultured cream

We make our yogurt and thick set cultured cream using the same method and often add a tablespoon of milk kefir for more microbial diversity. You can follow the same method to create either one. Both are unctuous, thick and delicious, with live cultures of probiotic bacteria that support gut microbial health. The yogurt is an effective way to get probiotics on a daily basis, and it goes with almost any of the recipes in this book. We occasionally serve the cream with donuts or apple pie.

Studies in humans show that supplementing your diet with live-cultured yogurt increases the abundance of probiotic bacteria *Lactobacillus* and *Bifidobacterium*, which help protect from invasions by pathogenic species, and also support the existence of bacteria that produce butyrate (see page 20). In particular, studies show that several types of *Lactobacillus* and *Bifidobacterium* present in yogurt can improve mood, depression, social anxiety, and stress resilience.

Making your own yogurt from a shop-bought live one is an excellent way to get lots of probiotics. You can then add more from other sources, such as kefir. Make sure your shop-bought yogurt is organic. Not all yogurts contain probiotics, so look for the words "contains live cultures" on the pot. Particular ones to look out for include *Bifidobacterium* species, *Lactobacillus acidophilus*, *L. casei*, and *L. bulgaricus*. Many commercially produced yogurts contain additives, including artificial flavorings and colorings, modified starches, fructose, and sweeteners, so avoid these.

In a heavy-based saucepan, heat the milk or cream over a medium heat until the temperature reaches 91°C (196°F), which is just below boiling point. Remove from the heat and leave to cool until the temperature falls to 46°C (115°F).

Pour the milk or cream into a bowl. Whisk in the cold live yogurt and kefir (if using). Cover the bowl with a clean dish towel and place it somewhere warm overnight, such as an airing cupboard. Alternatively, you can pour the contents into a warmed, wide-mouthed Thermos flask and seal.

If your yogurt/cultured cream is still too liquid in the morning, leave it wrapped up in the warm for another couple of hours. When it reaches the right thickness, transfer it to a sterilized container with a lid; a heavy glass jar is ideal. Store at 5°C (41°F). It will keep for up to two weeks in the fridge. Do remember to reserve some to use for the next batch.

# Crème pâtissière

We re-thought crème pâtissière. The traditional French version is exquisite, but it is biologically dead. To nourish the gut, this recipe takes a classic formula and applies the core principle of including a probiotic with each bake, inoculating it with kefir and letting it ferment overnight. At the School, we use a particular kefir that has over 14 probiotics in it and includes almost all the bacteria listed on pages 22–23. The result is a complex and probiotic-rich filling for donuts and pastries. It's also delicious simply dolloped on the side of any cake or bake.

You can replace the malt with sugar if you prefer, or if you don't like sugar, you can leave it out. You could also replace the kefir with a live yogurt.

▶ **INGREDIENTS**

3 egg yolks
60g (2¼oz) light spraymalt
20g (¾oz) cornstarch
250ml (9fl oz) whole milk
1 vanilla bean, scraped out
14g (½oz) sweet butter
40g (1½oz) thick live yogurt or kefir

*You will need a food thermometer*

▶ **SCHEDULE**

Day 1  8pm      Make crème
        8.30pm  Ferment overnight
Day 2  8am      Refrigerate until needed

In a bowl, whisk together the egg yolks and spraymalt. Add the cornstarch and mix well.

Heat the milk in a saucepan over a medium heat. When it boils, pour the milk into the egg mixture along with the vanilla bean. Mix well, then transfer the mixture to the saucepan and bring to the boil again, whisking all the while. It should now be nice and thick. After 4–5 minutes, remove it from the heat and stir in the butter. Now leave the mixture to cool to 30°C (86°F).

Once cooled, inoculate with the yogurt by whisking it in. Pour the mixture into a suitable sterilized container and cover closely, keeping any air out. Allow to cool completely. Leave aside overnight at 23°C (73°F) (the ambient temperature of the kitchen here), then refrigerate until needed. Use within 4–5 days. This becomes sourer as it ages.

Let the crème pâtissière down with a tablespoon of water if it is too thick to pipe.

## Variation

For the mille feuille (see page 176), donuts (see page 181), and any of the recipes in this book, you can use this crème pâtissière to make Diplomat cream. Lightly whip 200g cold cultured cream (see page 72) into medium peaks, then add 75g of crème pâtissière to your whipped cream. Leave it in the fridge overnight. Use in place of crème pâtissière.

# Malted orange labneh

We use variations of labneh to accompany all our bakes at the School—it goes with almost anything. It is especially good as a topping for scones. It's also a simple, inexpensive way to increase both your protein intake and your probiotics, and can be made with sheep or goat's milk as well as cow's. For more information about the principle of inoculating yogurt with strain-specific bacteria, see page 65.

**▶ INGREDIENTS**

100g (3½oz) kefir
100g (3½oz) spraymalt
1kg (2lb 4oz) high-protein, thick yogurt
   (e.g. Greek yogurt)
3g (1/10oz) sea salt
finely grated zest of 2 oranges

## Variations

**This labneh recipe is very versatile. You can create a range of diverse labnehs, for example:**

**MALTY CHOCOLATE LABNEH**
Substitute the orange zest for 1 tablespoon raw cacao powder, sifted.

**FESTIVE LABNEH**
Substitute the orange zest for the zest of 2 clementines and add 1 level tablespoon cinnamon.

**MOROCCAN LABNEH**
Omit the orange zest. Top the plain labneh with 2 tablespoons finely chopped fresh mint. Drizzle generously with pomegranate syrup and scatter some chopped pistachios on top.

Pour the kefir into a bowl. Sift in the spraymalt and mix until blended into the liquid. Spraymalt is hygroscopic and will form lumps if you act too fast. Stir until the spraymalt is well incorporated and the mixture is smooth and glossy.

Add the yogurt and salt to the mixture and stir well.

Place a sieve over another mixing bowl. Wet a clean dish towel and line a fine mesh strainer with it. Pour the yogurt mixture into the towel. Leave the mixture on your worksurface to drain overnight or for 12 hours.

Your labneh is ready when the yogurt has turned into a thick, creamy spread which releases easily from the cloth. If it's still sticking to the cloth, it's not ready.

Pick up the towel containing the labneh and turn the labneh out into a bowl. Add the orange zest and stir well one more time. Store in a sealed, sterilized container in the fridge. It will keep for 4–5 days.

Tip If the labneh has set too thickly to spread, add a drop of water and mix well.

MAKES 400–500G (14OZ–1LB 2OZ)
DIVERSITY SCORE 3

▶ INGREDIENTS

1 litre fresh heavy cream
100g good quality yogurt or kefir
4g sea salt

# Cultured butter

Culturing butter makes it easier to digest and is an instant way to increase your probiotics.

Mix together the cream and yogurt in a clean bowl. Leave it somewhere warm for 12 hours or overnight. The warmth allows it to ferment.

Put this mixture in the fridge to chill. Then whip it really hard until it splits into butter and buttermilk, and turns yellow. Put back into the fridge to solidify. This makes it easier to handle. Drain, separating the buttermilk (which can be used in recipes or drunk) and add the salt.

# Auntie's ghee

Ghee is butter that has had the milk solids removed. It has huge advantages over using butter, because if you bake butter at a high temperature, the milk solids cook and the smoking point drops, which can give a burnt flavor to your baked goods.

I learned this recipe from one of my Saudi Arabian students. This technique added such beautiful aromas to our bakes that now it's the only ghee we use. The ghee has a nutty, butterscotch flavor and a beautifully complex fragrance from all the spices.

MAKES ABOUT 500G (1LB 2OZ)   DIVERSITY SCORE 8

▶ INGREDIENTS

1 tablespoon cumin
1 tablespoon ground coriander
1 tablespoon ground fennel
500g (1lb 2oz) butter
1 tablespoon fenugreek
1 tablespoon ground turmeric
1 tablespoon curry leaves (optional)
2 tablespoons wholegrain flour

Tip We almost always use this ghee to grease our baking tins at the School. It's especially good for the Farinata recipe (page 125).

In a dry saucepan, lightly toast the cumin, coriander and fennel over a low heat. Add the butter.

As the butter melts, add the fenugreek, turmeric and curry leaves (if using). The butter will start to bubble and separate, and the whey from the butter will come up to the surface. Add the flour, a little at a time.

As the whey rises, skim it off by gently scooping it away with a spoon. (Save it to add to mashed potatoes or drizzle over broccoli.)

Keep cooking the butter until it turns clear and the milk solids, flour and spices sink to the bottom of the saucepan. At this point, it's essentially clarified butter. Let it cool, but while it is still liquid strain it through a cheesecloth into a clean container or bowl and allow to set. Store in the fridge and use as necessary. It will keep for up to 3 months in a sealed container such as a jam jar.

# Sourdough vanilla ice cream

**This is most definitely a recipe for grown-ups. The trick is the combination of a slightly salted, rich, creamy, honey and vanilla base, with the fantastic crunch of dried sourdough croutons. You will only achieve this by making sure that your sourdough is well and truly dry, and that it retains its characteristics within the ice cream by adding it at the very last minute. Use sourdough bread that is at least a couple of days old, so it has had the chance to develop its full sourness.**

▶ **INGREDIENTS**

400ml (14fl oz) Cultured cream (page 72)

5 egg yolks

400ml (14fl oz) full-fat milk

1 Ndali vanilla bean (split lengthways)

3 tablespoons fresh kefir or live yogurt

75g (2¾oz) raw honey

a pinch of sea salt

150g (5½oz) sourdough rye bread*, toasted (see method) and chopped into 1cm squares

50g (1¾oz) molasses

30g (1oz) sesame seeds, toasted

*We use the Russian Rye recipe from page 127 of my book *The Sourdough School*.

Put the cream, egg yolks, milk and vanilla bean into a large saucepan. Whisk briefly to thoroughly disperse the egg yolks.

Place the saucepan over a low heat and whisk continuously. This is a moment to contemplate life, listen to the radio, or generally cogitate. It is not a moment to rush, or you will scramble the eggs, and that is impossible to reverse. The mixture will take about 15 minutes to thicken, which will happen just at the point it begins to boil. Set to one side until fully cooled, then add the kefir and honey. Add a pinch of salt, and taste for the sweet–saltiness balance. Leave on the worksurface overnight to ferment at an ambient temperature.

The next day, preheat the oven to 150°C/300°F/Gas Mark 2. Pop the sourdough squares on a flat baking tray and bake for 10–15 minutes until golden. Set aside until fully dried and completely crunchy.

Once the cream mixture has fermented, pour it into a suitable round-bottomed container and place it in the freezer. Over the next 1½ hours, remove the ice cream from the freezer every 30 minutes and whisk to get a smooth result. On the third or fourth whisk, as the ice cream is getting thick, stir in the sourdough croutons, then the molasses and sesame seeds. At this point, transfer the ice cream into a loaf tin lined with greaseproof paper. Continue to freeze until frozen.

The ice cream will keep in the freezer for up to 3 months. To serve, remove from the freezer for 10 minutes to allow the ice cream to soften a little before scooping.

This ice cream is delicious spooned between my Chocolate chip biscuits (page 138).

▶ **INGREDIENTS**

650g (1lb 7oz) fruit of your choice,
   pitted/stoned and cut into chunks
80–200g (2¾–7 oz) sugar (such as demerara,
   raw cane, muscovado, or honey or maple syrup)
   depending on the sweetness of the fruit
   (see below)

*You will need two sterilized 500g (1lb 2oz) jam jars*

## How to judge the sugar needed for fruit compotes

My fresh fruit compotes are much lower in sugar than a regular marmalade or jam. I like the fruit to play the main part in the sweetness and flavor of my compotes, while the sugar is used only to balance. Some fruit is so naturally sweet, it doesn't even need any sugar.

So, before you begin to make your compote, make sure you taste the fruit. Try and connect to your sense of taste and ask yourself how much of a natural sweetness is already there? It's very much up to you how much sugar you decide to use. This recipe is only a guideline, more of a technique than a typical recipe.

For very sweet fruits, such as apricots, nectarines or plums, I use 60–80g (2 ¼–3 oz) sugar, whereas tart fruits, such as redcurrants, Morello cherries or rhubarb, I might use up to 250g (9 oz) sugar, or more if this isn't enough. Add the sugar a little at a time and taste as you go, stopping when you get to the level of sweetness you like.

Tip If the compote doesn't thicken, stir in about 1 tablespoon of chia seeds.

# Fresh fruit compote

Berries play a key role in nourishing the gut, and we grow them throughout the School gardens: raspberries, cherries, strawberries, gooseberries, blackberries and blackcurrants. Our senses tell us that these pigment-rich berries are important for our health. They are rich, sweet and juicy, and the first thing we did when we moved here was plant the garden full of fruit. In our first weeks here, my mother bought me a mulberry tree and we planted it right outside the door. As we picked the very first berries a year later, my husband told me that my grandchildren would one day do the same.

That tree is quite a size now and, in the warmth of late summer, our students stand under the tree, picking and eating the abundance of warm berries straight from the branches. The skin, flesh and seeds of these berries have an abundance of phytochemicals, vitamins, fibre and trace elements. They contain high levels polyphenols (page 29), which perform important antioxidant and anti-inflammatory roles for human health. Importantly, most of the polyphenols in our diet are not actually extracted directly by our small intestine, but are made available to us by the action of probiotic bacteria in the colon, especially *Bifidobacterium*. Growing evidence also pinpoints possible roles for these polyphenol-rich berries in supporting brain health, cognitive function and mood, and possibly even helping to alleviate depression and anxiety too.

---

Put the fruit in a saucepan over a medium heat. Add a splash of water to prevent the fruit from burning. When the fruit begins to bubble, reduce the heat immediately and let simmer until the fruit softens (different fruits will take different lengths of time, so keep checking) and the liquid has boiled down.

Stir in the sugar, honey, or syrup a little at a time, tasting between additions (let it cool on the spoon before tasting!) to get the right amount. Make sure it dissolves completely. Let the compote cook through for another 3–5 minutes.

Scoop the compote into the sterilized jam jars, using a funnel to avoid spoilage. Screw the lids on and leave to cool. Store your compote in the fridge and use within 7 days.

## Honey

Several *in vivo* and *in vitro* studies on altering the composition of the gut microbiota by increasing the growth of probiotic *Lactobacilli* and *Bifidobacterium*, have primarily focused on prebiotic fructo-oligosaccharides. Honey contains potentially prebiotic oligosaccharides and antibacterial components. Early research is looking at how these two components can potentially synergistically enhance the probiotic efficacy against pathogens in the gut. In addition, some studies have reported that benefits of unpasteurized honey may enhance probiotic persistence in the GI tract, elevated levels of SCFAs (page 20), and increased resistance to pathogens.

MAKES ABOUT1.5 LITRES (2¾ PINTS)
**DIVERSITY SCORE** 4

### ▶ INGREDIENTS

30 white elderflower heads
750g (1lb 10oz) superfine sugar
1.5 litres (2¾ pints) water
4 tablespoons hibiscus flowers
3–4 30cm (12-inch) stems fresh angelica, chopped (optional)
zest and juice of 2 lemons

Tip **Remember to sterilize your equipment and allow the syrups to cool before adding them to the bottles.**

## Syrups

These syrups are absolutely key to the recipes in this book. They also form the base of our water kefirs.

We do not totally avoid sugar at the School, but we do actively reduce it wherever possible. Often people need to avoid sugar, and one of the most difficult things about having a digestive or health issue is a feeling of separation, of not being able to eat together. It can be distressing when friends and family come together and you have to refuse food or explain that you are avoiding sugar. These syrups allow us to individualize all our bakes and be flexible about how much sweetness we add.

The sugar that is used in our recipes is almost completely consumed by the LAB (page 105) during fermentation and increases the acidity. This means the cakes are not sweet. Using these syrups adds sweetness and creates a contrast between sweet and sour, which intensifies the flavors. The syrup can be added at the end of a bake and the quantity adjusted as required by the individual—or it can be left out altogether. A drizzle of syrup also significantly extends the shelf life of your bakes by up to 48 hours.

These syrups are core to increasing levels of polyphenols. I often use them to increase the probiotics by mixing them with a little live vinegar (1 tablespoon of live vinegar to 5 tablespoons syrup).

## Elderflower & hibiscus syrup

The addition of hibiscus flowers gives a gorgeous blush.

Shake the elderflowers to ensure there are no insects hiding among their petals. Trim any stems and leaves and discard.

Put the sugar and water in a saucepan over a medium heat and stir until all the sugar has dissolved. Allow to cool.

When the sugar-and-water mixture reaches bath temperature, add the elderflowers, hibiscus, angelica, and lemon zest and juice. Stir well, cover, and leave for 24 hours at ambient temperature, stirring occasionally.

Strain the syrup through a piece of cheesecloth or an old, clean, cotton dish towel in a colander, ensuring that none of the bits get through. Decant into sterilized bottles. This will keep in the fridge for 6 months.

MAKES ABOUT 1.5 LITRES (2¾ PINTS)
**DIVERSITY SCORE** 3

▶ **INGREDIENTS**
10–15 fig leaves
1.5 litres (2¾ pints) water
750g (1lb 10oz) superfine sugar
3–4 30cm (12-inch) stems fresh angelica,
    chopped (optional)
zest and juice of 2 lemons

MAKES ABOUT 700ML (1¼ PINTS)
**DIVERSITY SCORE** 3

▶ **INGREDIENTS**
zest and juice of 4 oranges
150g (5½oz) root ginger, grated
500ml (18 fl oz) water
250ml (9oz) raw honey

MAKES ABOUT 750ML (1⅓ PINTS)
**DIVERSITY SCORE** 3

▶ **INGREDIENTS**
zest and juice of 6 lemons
a handful of lemon verbena, lemon thyme or
    lemon balm leaves (optional)
500ml (18 fl oz) water
250g (9oz) raw honey

MAKES ABOUT 900ML (1½ PINTS)
**DIVERSITY SCORE** 3

▶ **INGREDIENTS**
600g (1lb 5oz) cherries
4 cloves
500ml (18 fl oz) water
250g (9oz) raw honey

# Fig leaf syrup

Follow the recipe on the previous page, replacing the elderflowers and hibiscus with 10–15 fig leaves.

# Honey, ginger & orange syrup

Perfect for the festive season.

Follow the same method as for the Crab apple & rosehip syrup (see page 88).

# Lemon syrup

This is my favorite syrup. The herbs are optional but add a layer of complexity that I really enjoy.

Follow the same method as for the Crab apple & rosehip syrup (see page 88).

# Cherry syrup

Cherries have significant levels of anthocyanins, polyphenols that specifically feed Akkermansia (page 22).

Follow the same method as for the Crab apple & rosehip syrup (see page 88).

# Crab apple & rosehip syrup

Both crab apples and rosehips are rich in polyphenols and flavor. They add complexity and an aromatic, sweet tartness.

MAKES ABOUT 700ML (1¼ PINTS)
DIVERSITY SCORE 3

▶ INGREDIENTS

500g (1lb 2oz) crab apples, left whole
100g (3½oz) rosehips
500ml (18 fl oz) water
250g (9 oz) raw honey

Place all the ingredients except the honey in a large saucepan and bring to the boil. Reduce the heat and simmer until the liquid has reduced by a third.

Allow to cool, using a fork to lightly mash the apples and rosehips to create a pulp as they cool. When the mixture reaches below 30°C (86°F), add the honey and stir well to combine (adding the honey at this temperature allows it to retain its microbial benefits). Strain and decant into a sterilized glass bottle. This will keep in the fridge for up to 3 months.

# Wild strawberry & mint syrup

Mint is appreciated for its fresh, cooling flavors, which work well infused into any number of dishes. It has even been used throughout the ages to aid digestion. This is thanks to the oils it contains, especially menthol and menthone, which are effective for relieving abdominal cramps and gas. A number of studies indicate that peppermint oil can help with IBS and has less adverse effects than antispasmodic medication. In fact, a small study even showed that the essential oils in peppermint could prevent the postoperative nausea that is common in patients who have woken up from surgery. *In vitro* research also indicates that peppermint oil has antibacterial properties that can target pathogenic microbes like salmonella, shigella, and *E. coli*.

MAKES ABOUT 800–900ML (1½–1¾ PINTS)
DIVERSITY SCORE 3

▶ INGREDIENTS

600g (1lb 5oz) fresh strawberries
250g (9oz) coconut sugar
500ml (18 fl oz) water
a large bunch of fresh mint

Place all the ingredients in a large saucepan and bring to the boil. Reduce the heat and simmer until the liquid has reduced by a third.

Allow to cool, then strain and decant into a sterilized glass bottle. This will keep in the fridge for up to 3 months.

# Wild vinegar

We make our own vinegars at the School. They are so easy and delicious. The easiest one to start with is apple cider vinegar. We use them in salad dressings and with shrubs (simply dilute to taste with sparkling water), which is another easy way of getting probiotics into your everyday diet. You'll see I haven't been able to provide an exact "makes" quantity for this recipe because it doesn't use exact measurements, but as a guide, the quantity of vinegar produced will be about 20 per cent less than the quantity of water used.

▶ **INGREDIENTS**

6–8 apples, with core and peel (stem removed)
6–8 teaspoons raw honey or unrefined sugar,
    to taste
water, to cover

Wipe the apples with a clean, damp kitchen cloth and cut any bad bits out. Chop each of the apples into 6–8 pieces. Pop them into a clean, sterilized wide-mouthed jar.

Take a jug of water and add the honey or sugar to the water gradually, tasting as you go until you get the level of sweetness equivalent to a sweet tea. Pour enough of this sweetened water over the apples to cover them. Cover the jar with a piece of clean cotton and secure it with an elastic band.

Leave the jar on the side in the kitchen for 1 month.

After 1 month, strain the contents of the jar through a piece of cheesecloth folded several times. Pour the strained liquid into a sterilized bottle and leave it to ferment at room temperature for another 2–3 weeks, giving it a shake every few days and "burping" twice a day every day (or it will explode—see Tip on page 92). You'll know when it's ready because it will taste like vinegar. The vinegar will be cloudy to begin with, but it will settle.

## Variations

**We make several other vinegar flavors using the same method:**

### CHERRY VINEGAR

Replace the apples with cherries.

### PEAR & GINGER VINEGAR

Replace the apples with pears and a 15–20cm (6–8-inch) piece of fresh ginger, sliced.

### MIRABELLE PLUM VINEGAR

Replace the apples with mirabelle plums.

### HEDGEROW BLACKBERRY VINEGAR

Replace the apples with wild blackberries.

### ROSEHIP & RASPBERRY VINEGAR

Replace the apples with rosehips and raspberries. Soft fruit vinegars tend to ferment a little faster, so adjust the times accordingly.

# Sourdough fizz

Sourdough fizz is a sparkling, fruity, acidic, slightly sweet, aromatic fermented drink. We make a variety of different sourdough fizzes at the School, and often serve it alongside our cakes, bakes, breads and puddings. It also makes a good afternoon refreshment on its own. One of my favourite sourdough fizzes is Chamomile and honey (see Variations).

To make the sourdough fizz, you'll need a ratio of about 1 part fruit syrup to 4 parts water. By then adding the starter, you are turning it into a natural probiotic. Let me give you a small but crucial piece of advice. Your starter has to be in good health and not contaminated in any way. I advise you to use a refreshed starter that has been allowed to then rest in the fridge for 2–3 days to sour. It should have a vinegary tang to it. You want it to have a low pH because unwanted and potentially pathogenic bacteria will not survive in an acidic starter. Likewise, ensure that you have clean hands and use sterilized bottles. That way, you can be confident that you are culturing just the beneficial microbes.

The principle for making sourdough fizz is incredibly simple. Mix the water and syrup together in a sterilized 1-litre (1¾ pint) bottle and give it a good shake to get the syrup evenly distributed throughout the liquid.

Then you need to add a form of inoculation; we use our sourdough starter. You only need the tiniest amount: usually around ¼ teaspoon (3–4g). Close the lid on the bottle and give the mixture another vigorous shake. This isn't merely to disperse the sourdough starter through the cordial. It also helps to oxygenate the water; and yeasts need some oxygen to reproduce.

Leave the bottle on the worksurface, with the lid on, for about 3 days (in the summer, it can take as little as 2 days). After a few days of anaerobic fermentation at room temperature, it will be ready.

The critical thing to remember whenever you have a bottle fermenting is its potential to explode. I'm really not exaggerating! You need to "burp" it to release the build-up of gases generated by the fermentation regularly; otherwise, you risk a spectacular explosion (see Tip).

Once your fizz is fermented and is effervescing gently, you can pop it in the fridge. It's still worth burping the bottle every 2–3 days to start with; it will eventually calm down, but you'll still need to burp it once every 2–3 weeks once it has settled down. It will keep for about 4–6 weeks and gets progressively sourer as time goes on.

## ▶ INGREDIENTS

200g (7oz) organic Fruit syrup (pages 84–89, or you can use shop-bought cordial syrup, but look for one that is produced and sweetened with only a pure form of sugar)

800ml (1½ pints) water, left to stand for 20 minutes to dechlorinate

4g sourdough starter (pages 106–109)

*You will need a sterilized 1-litre (1¾-pint) bottle*

# Variations

### CHAMOMILE & HONEY SOURDOUGH FIZZ

Combine 750ml (1¹/₃ pints) cooled chamomile tea with 150g (5½oz) raw honey in a sterilized bottle. Add 4g sourdough starter and leave to ferment as right. Chamomile is a powerful anti-inflammatory. It's well documented as having a positive effect on anxiety.

### WHEY & HONEY SOURDOUGH FIZZ

Combine 500ml (18fl oz) whey with 100g (3½oz) raw honey in a sterilized bottle. Add 3g sourdough starter and leave to ferment as right.

## Tip
I suggest two things to help you remember to "burp" your fizz while it's fermenting. First, leave the bottle where you will see it often (in the School, we leave it next to the coffee machine). Secondly, set an alarm or reminder on your phone as a back-up. This can save you a lot of mess. There was a very memorable blackcurrant fizz explosion at the School once that reached several metres across the room and took 8 or 9 hours to clean up.

# Cherry & Earl Grey kvass

Kvass is one of my favourite ways to use up leftover sourdough. It is a traditional Baltic and Slavonic drink, originally made from the black and rye breads especially popular in Russia, Ukraine, Georgia, Latvia and Lithuania. It has a tangy, earthy, malted taste, quite similar to a deep, dark beer. It can be layered with other flavors, with herbs like mint or fruits such as berries and raisins. Some alcohol is present, but like kombucha, it is lacto-fermented.

## ▶ INGREDIENTS

about 300g (10½oz) sourdough crusts (either rye or wholegrain), toasted if you like (see Tip)
130g (4¾oz) sugar (we use coconut sugar)
30g (1oz) molasses (optional, for a deeper, richer, almost beer-like flavor)
2 litres (3½ pints) Earl Grey tea, at about 28–30°C (82–86°F)
1 vanilla bean (optional)
1 tablespoon sourdough starter (pages 106–109)

## ▶ FOR THE SECONDARY FERMENTATION

70g (2½oz) Cherry syrup (page 87) or fruit syrup of your choice

*You will need a large glass jar (large enough to fit all the ingredients with room to spare for fermentation), cheesecloth and 2 x 1-litre (1¾-pint) sterilized glass or plastic bottles*

## Variations

You could use fruit juices instead of tea, or use one of the other syrups (pages 84–88) instead of the Cherry syrup.

## Tip

I sometimes toast the sourdough crusts first, to accentuate the Maillard (see page 186) reaction and get richer, toffee-flavored notes.

Put the sourdough crusts into the glass jar. Add the sugar and molasses, if using, and stir to combine. Pour the tea into the jar, then add the vanilla bean and the sourdough starter and stir. Cover your jar with a loose-fitting lid and leave it to sit on the kitchen worksurface for about 2 days at ambient temperature. It's a good idea to put a tray underneath the jar because it can bubble over. Also watch out for fruit flies. They are attracted to the smell of fermentation, so keep the lid loose, but still covering the jar so they can't get in.

Once your kvass has really started to fizz, it is ready to drink as it is, if you wish. It should taste sour and the sugar should have pretty much disappeared. I prefer to give it a secondary fermentation. Strain the liquid through a cheesecloth overnight, discarding all the bits (this is a personal preference; some people like to see the bits at the bottom). Add the syrup to the strained liquid.

Pour the liquid into your bottles. It's difficult to say exactly how much it will makes because it depends how much liquid the bread absorbs. Put on the lids and leave them in a relatively warm environment (about 21–22°C/70–72°F) for about 24–36 hours. You absolutely must "burp" the bottles twice a day, because if you don't the gas will build up during this secondary fermentation, and you could end up with an explosion. So set an alarm to remind you. Hold the bottle over the kitchen sink as you release the gas and, if you're using glass bottles, have a clean dish towel wrapped around your hand as you do it, just in case the bottle shatters. If it's your first time making this kvass, use a plastic bottle, just to be on the safe side.

After 24 hours, the kvass should be really fizzing away. If the room temperature is colder, it may take up to 36 hours. At this stage the kvass is ready. Store it in the fridge, but remember to continue burping it at least once a day; I do it every morning as the kettle boils for my first cup of coffee.

# Chocolate, almond & hazelnut spread

Chocolate has high levels of phytonutrients and polyphenols (pages 29–30). It is a feast for *Bifidobacterium* and *Lactobacillus*: levels of both are increased when you consume bittersweet chocolate, which actually helps maintain balance in the gut.

▶ **INGREDIENTS**

125g (4½ oz) whole almonds

125g (4½ oz) whole hazelnuts

1 tablespoon walnut or hazelnut oil

240g (8½oz) confectioner's sugar

150g (5½oz) bittersweet chocolate, melted

150g (5½oz) sweet butter, at room temperature

*You will need a sterilized 500g (1lb 2oz) jar*

Preheat the oven to 160°C/325°F/Gas Mark 3.

Scatter the almonds on one baking sheet and the hazelnuts on another. Roast the almonds for 10 minutes and the hazelnuts for 8 minutes. Keep an eye on the nuts as they roast and remove them from the oven as soon as they start to turn dark brown.

Let the nuts cool, and once they are cool enough to touch, rub them gently between your fingers to remove the skins.

Transfer the roasted nuts to a food processor and grind to a fine powder. Add the oil and confectioner's sugar and pulse until you have a smooth paste.

Scrape the paste into a large mixing bowl. Add the melted chocolate and stir to combine, then stir in the butter.

Transfer to a sterilized 500g (1lb 2oz) jar. This will keep in the fridge for up to 2 months.

## Variations

### VEGAN CHOCOLATE, HAZELNUT AND ALMOND SPREAD

To make a vegan version, roast and grind the almonds and hazelnuts as right, then add 4 big Medjool dates (about 75g/2¾oz) and pulse in a food processor. Stir in the melted bittersweet chocolate and 100g (3½oz) coconut oil, and a pinch of salt to taste, then transfer to a jar as right.

# Notes

# The sourdough process

# Borrowing digestion

## My part in the story

As someone who has spent the majority of my adult life working with and researching the transformative process of fermenting grains, my focus has been on understanding this process, how it affects the nutrition and digestibility of bread, and how that makes us feel.

My own gut microbiome was severely compromised in my early twenties. It took me many years to discover why I couldn't easily digest non-sourdough baked goods. I was told in the early 1990s that I had "leaky gut". To be frank, I was initially revolted by the idea that I was full of microbes. It took over 20 years to fully comprehend the extent of the damage done to my gut. In 2016, Professor Tim Spector's team tested my biome to discover that I had less than 2 per cent diversity.

## Why stop at bread?

In the meantime, I worked out that I could "borrow" digestion. A sourdough starter pot is a sort of mini version of what goes on in our gut. As a micro version of our own digestive system, it uses many of the same families of lactic acid bacteria (LAB) that are on our skin and in our guts. It makes sense, really, that sourdough is easier to digest, because the dough has already been partially "digested" before you even eat it. It is also logical, when you look at the evidence, that your food is then more nutritious; the breakdown during fermentation makes the fibre, polyphenols, vitamins, and minerals more bioavailable, and degrades the gluten. This is the key reason that our digestive system has a much easier time with sourdough, so it is both more nourishing and less inflammatory.

Inoculating Botanical Blend no. 3 with a starter—fermentation is pre-digestion.

On the one hand, much of my work has seen me buried underneath piles of scientific papers, looking at the exact mechanisms and specific changes elicited by fermentation; and on the other, I was baking and applying my findings to the bread that I made. But why stop at bread? Sourdough is a process, not just a type of bread. I started using the sourdough process to ferment cakes, puddings, and pastry, making simple bakes that were a joy to eat.

## Fermentation changes everything

There is a clear link between digestion and the way we feel. When I began teaching, it became evident that I was not the only one who had digestive issues. People who attended my classes from far and wide often reported self-diagnosed gluten intolerances. They would tell me that they could eat sourdough products without any digestive discomfort, and that they felt better both physically and mentally.

I don't have an explanation as to exactly why their mood improved. There are many mechanisms that may contribute to why people feel happier and healthier when eating sourdough, including the reduction in irritable bowel syndrome (IBS) symptoms, better control of blood sugar, higher levels of fibre—as well as the sheer joy of baking. However, in light of research that has shown that individuals with gastrointestinal disorders are far more likely to have a higher prevalence of negative mental symptoms, including depression and anxiety, and that people with depression commonly report gastrointestinal symptoms such as diarrhea, constipation, and bloating, it doesn't seem so surprising that eating food that is more easily tolerated by the digestive system might ease some of these digestive malaise symptoms associated with mental health issues.

# There are still more questions than answers

Despite researching for many years, I still have more questions than answers, but one of the things that is becoming clearer is that mental health and stress are linked to intestinal permeability, and intestinal permeability is linked to an immune response to gluten.

So:
1. Does the fermentation of flour break down gluten to the extent that it prevents the proteins from triggering an immune response?
2. Do the increased nutrition and higher levels of fibre help to restore the gut flora's balance?
3. Considering the change in nutritional profile, could this long, slow fermentation process be the missing link in the optimal functioning of our gut?
4. Is fermentation the answer to reducing inflammation?

## Gluten degradation

Certainly, during sourdough fermentation several important things are happening, which come about through the biochemical activities of the LAB and wild yeasts. Firstly, fermentation facilitates the breakdown of macronutrients, including gluten and other proteins within wheat resulting in a "reduced gluten load", according to a 2004 study by renowned sourdough microbiologist Marco Gobbetti. The study indicated that long, slow sourdough fermentation modifies parts of both the glutenin and gliadin proteins that make up gluten.

I suspect that this gluten degradation may be one of the key mechanisms that means people with Non-Coeliac Gluten Sensitivity (NCGS) can digest sourdough more easily than other breads, although more studies are needed to investigate this.

# Reduction in symptoms of IBS

FODMAPs (Fermentable Oligosaccharides, Disaccharides, Monosaccharides and Polyols) are a collection of poorly absorbed simple and complex carbohydrates found in various foods, including wheat. After digestion of a meal, these components pass through our digestive tract unchanged and are either fermented by colonic bacteria releasing gas, or expelled altogether. For some people, when FODMAPs are eaten, they can cause symptoms that include bloating, pain and diarrhea, especially in people who have IBS or a sensitive gut. The long, slow fermentation process of wheat contributes significantly to how easily digested whole wheat is compared to fast-fermented bread. Research has shown that the long fermentation process effectively diminishes the levels of FODMAP carbohydrates by 90 per cent, making it easier for people to enjoy eating the most basic of everyday foods.

# Controlling blood sugar and mood

There is evidence suggesting that the production of acids during sourdough fermentation can help slow down the rate of assimilation of carbohydrates, and thus reduce the risk of spikes in blood sugar levels. As blood sugar levels drop, levels of the stress hormone cortisol increase, so blood sugar management is a major factor to consider when looking at diet and the influence of what we eat on our stress levels (Polese et al., 2018; Anita Mofidi et al., 2012). Wholegrain, stoneground flour has also been shown to further slow down blood sugar response.

# Increasing resistant starch

The LAB involved in sourdough fermentation have also been shown to increase the levels of resistant starch in bread and other baked products. Resistant starch is an important component of a healthy diet (page 11). Unlike other carbohydrates, it cannot be digested without the help of microbes. It passes through to the intestine, where it provides a source of food for the gut microbes.

As the resistant starch is broken down by the microbes, short chain fatty acids (SCFAs, page 20) are released. Analysis of sourdough has shown levels of resistant starch to be 20–30 per cent higher than that found in breads that are traditionally baked using just baker's yeast. This in part explains the better post-prandial glucose response (blood sugar) observed in studies when eating wholegrain sourdough.

## A game changer

When you look at the whole picture, it seems obvious to me that the increased support to the gut microbiome through increased retention of vitamins and accessibility of phenolic compounds is a game changer. Pre-clinical studies have shown that the fermentation process increases the bioavailability of key nutrients that we know nourish the microbes in the gut, including fibre (see Chapter 2) and phenolic compounds (page 29) (Calinoiu and Vodnar, 2018).

Fermentation also increases levels of folate and thiamin (B vitamins) during the baking process of both wheat and rye, and there is also evidence showing improved retention of riboflavin (another B vitamin) and vitamin E, mainly present in wheat germ.

## Increased bioavailability of minerals

One of the enzymes that gets activated during the extended fermentation process is phytase, which is a phytic acid-degrading enzyme. Phytase draws minerals to it, like a magnet, by neutralising phytic acid there is up to an 80 per cent increase in the bioavailability of minerals.

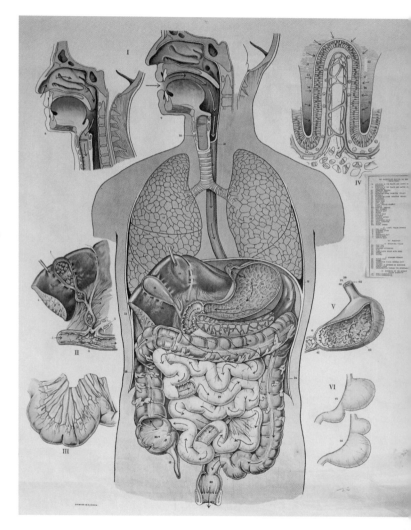

Simply slowing down and taking the time to bake, appreciate, and share bread you have made can change the way you feel and how your digestive system reacts. If you are under a lot of stress, your digestive system is compromised because all vital functions are directed to running away from a threat, not digesting your food.

# The amazing work of enzymes

Sugar is needed for fermentation, but flour only contains a very small amount of sugar, about 1–2 per cent. This is not enough to make dough rise. Starch is a more stable way for a plant to store energy, but in order for it to be used to feed an emerging plant, it must be broken down into sugar. It is this breakdown and availability of simple sugars that helps sourdough to ferment. This is the work of the enzymes. It is key to understanding sourdough.

## This breakdown is the work of enzymes

Most enzymes are simple proteins. An enzyme is a large molecule that catalyses a biological reaction. Enzymes speed up a reaction by reducing whatever energy barrier is preventing it from happening quickly and easily. Each enzyme has a very specific job to do and only interacts with the molecules it works on, ignoring all others.

In sourdough bread making, the enzyme that turns complex starches into simple sugars is called amylase. Amylase occurs naturally in wheat flour, and the amount varies according to the weather and specific harvesting conditions of the wheat. Amylase has a preferred pH of about 7 and it begins its work as you add water at the start of fermentation. The maltose molecules are separated into two glucose molecules, and it is glucose that the wild yeast and other LAB consume to produce the by-products that transform flour and water into leavened bread. Amylase is key to the LAB making oligosaccharides (page 26).

There are more enzymes, but the other two that we are most interested in are proteolytic enzymes and phytase. Proteolytic enzymes break down proteins, i.e. gluten. Phytase breaks down phytic acid. Both prefer a lower pH and so they become more active later on during the fermentation process.

Without these enzymes this transformation process wouldn't happen, and sourdough fermentation would be drastically impaired, if not impossible, because yeast requires simple sugars to produce carbon dioxide.

## How do enzymes work?

The simplified explanation in chemistry textbooks is called the "lock and key model". Each and every enzyme has a particular shape that fits together with the substrate, which is the molecule it breaks down. The enzyme essentially bonds to the substrate with a weaker chemical bond. The enzymes themselves remain intact and are not used up by the process of breaking down the bonds after the reaction occurs, so the original enzyme molecule is left intact and can continue to break down more bonds. They are relentless!

### WATER IS THE TRIGGER

Amylase is triggered when water is added to the flour. One of the reasons that doughs with higher hydration often ferment faster is because the more water there is, the more active the enzymes are. This increases the speed at which they break everything down. The water enables the amylase to penetrate the starch granules, and it has a far easier time accessing the starch in flour because starch granules are damaged during milling, providing more surface area. The result is increased sugar, which drives the fermentation.

# How do lactic acid bacteria affect the flavor?

There are many species of lactic acid bacteria (LAB). They can be categorized according to their by-products. Getting them to balance and colonize your ferment is the key to success. Without scientific analysis, you can't see exactly what's in your starter. However, starters will usually contain a balance of the below. This balance responds to the way you refresh your starter, what flour you use, and the type of yeast(s) that have colonized to form the symbiotic relationship that makes sourdough. There are so many possibilities. These are wild yeasts and bacteria that are part of the environment around you.

## Homofermentative LAB

These ferment glucose with lactic acid as their primary by-product. They produce a lighter, more yogurt-like flavor in bakes. Homofermentative LAB are the bacteria found in yogurt, an everyday food for many people. They are also found in kefir.

## Heterofermentative LAB

We specifically want to encourage these. They ferment glucose with lactic acid, ethanol/acetic acid and carbon dioxide ($CO_2$) as by-products. They produce a sourer taste, with flavors that are tangy and vinegary. It's perhaps a bit of a generalisation, because there are other factors involved in the acidification, but in general, bakes made with a predominantly heterofermentative balance are more broken down and more acidic, and so easier to digest.

## Facultatively heterofermentative LAB

There are also facultatively heterofermentative LAB. These produce mainly lactic acid but, in some cases, can also produce acetic.

---

**WHY ARE WE BUILDING UP ALL THESE BACTERIA IN THE SOURDOUGH JUST TO KILL THEM IN THE OVEN?**

The work that these bacteria do is key to the transformation of flour. The work they've done making the bakes more digestible and nutritious remains intact after they die. In addition, there is some evidence that dead LAB are positive because they have a prebiotic effect.

**A STARTER'S ACIDITY CAN PROTECT IT FROM PATHOGENS**

A starter kept in a clean, sterile jar and allowed to ferment correctly is acidic but sweet. I often describe it as a "members-only club", as the bacteria break down carbohydrates, fats and proteins and produce both lactic acid and acetic acid. As they produce acids, the pH of sourdough changes according to the stage of fermentation it is at, but in general it will have a pH of 3.5–5. This acidity is very important because it keeps out pathogenic microorganisms, such as *botulism* bacteria, *E. coli* bacteria, and spoilage fungi, which are unable to reproduce in an environment with a pH below 4.6.

This is especially important if you are going to use your starter to inoculate sourdough fizz or porridge, or use it as a probiotic because they're not cooked, which would naturally destroy these pathogens.

**INGREDIENTS**
Stoneground wholegrain flour
Water

**YOU'LL ALSO NEED SOME BASIC EQUIPMENT AND CONDITIONS**
A warm room. The ideal ambient temperature is a room where you are comfortable wearing just a t shirt (trousers are optional!)
A non-reactive container: a jam jar is good.
Make sure there are no other cultured foods nearby, or there will be cross-contamination and you might not get the microbes you want.

# Wild water

One of the fastest ways you can capture wild yeast is by using "wild water" made with fruit. On occasion, when we have tested wild fruit water there have been instances of unwanted bacterial growth. Allow your starter time to acidify, because the acidity makes the starter environment difficult for anything other than the LAB and wild yeast. It shouldn't be a problem with baking bread, because you're baking it at 200°C/400°F/Gas Mark 6 or higher. However, I would deter anyone from tasting a newly developed starter until it's got a history of acidifying a few times.

To make a wild fruit water, put 100g water in a jam jar with about 1 teaspoon sugar and 50–80g of any kind of organic fruit. Shake and leave it for 24 hours. Discard the fruit and use the water to make your starter. One of the most successful fruits I've used for wild water were green coffee beans sent to me by a student from India. The flavor was incredible. Rose hips, wild cherries, grapes or any stone fruit are fantastic for making wild water.

Note: I do not advise anyone with Crohn's disease or ulcerative colitis to use wild water, as it often contains *Saccharomyces cerevisiae*. 60–70 per cent of patients with Crohn's disease and 10–15 per cent of patients with ulcerative colitis test positive for antibodies against *S. cerevisiae*. I advise these people to use wholegrain rye to start their starter.

# How to make a sourdough starter from scratch

There are as many ways to start a starter as there are roads to Rome. Essentially, you are capturing wild yeast and LAB from the ingredients and the environment around you, nurturing them with food and warmth, and using the resulting starter as an inoculation with which to ferment your bakes. Richard Hart, one of the best sourdough bakers in the world, once described this process to me as "microbial farming".

## Creating your starter

To create your own sourdough starter, you just need two basic ingredients: organic, stoneground wholegrain flour and water.

**SCHEDULE**

| | | |
|---|---|---|
| Sunday | 8am | Mix together 110g tap water or wild water at 28°C and 100g wholegrain stoneground organic flour or Botanical Blend no.2 (page 55). Whisk the mixture vigorously to incorporate air: this encourages the yeast to develop. Cover with a breathable lid and leave at an ambient temperature. |
| Monday | 8am | Remove and discard 110g of the starter. Add 60g tap water at 28°C and 50g wholegrain stoneground organic flour or Botanical Blend no.2. Cover with a breathable lid and leave at an ambient temperature. |
| Monday | 8pm | Repeat |
| Tuesday | 8am | Repeat |
| Tuesday | 8pm | Repeat |
| Wednesday | 8am | Repeat |
| Wednesday | 8pm | Repeat |
| Thursday | 8am | Repeat |
| Thursday | 8pm | Repeat. By this time, your starter should be doubling in 4-5 hours. |

The starter is ready when it doubles in size about 5 hours after feeding. If your starter is not active by this point:
♦ Check that the flour you are using is actually organic
♦ check that the water you are adding is at 28°C
♦ Check that the room is warm enough—an ambient temperature of about 21°C.
♦ A cold starter or one made with grain covered in agrichemicals will not activate.

**It is now time to switch into maintenance mode.**

**DAY 1-2**

**DAY 3-4**

**DAY 4-5**

**DAY 5**

# How to refresh your starter: you are now in maintenance mode

# Sweet and sour starters

There are two different formulas for the sourdough starters used in the recipes throughout this book. They are both refreshed in exactly the same way, but one is sour while the other contains sugar and is sweet.

## Sour
The sour starter is thicker and more heterofermentative (page 105). It's the one I recommend for anyone who has digestive issues because it is acetic, which creates a higher level of acidity and breaks things down more.

## Sweet
I use the sweet starter when I want to reduce acidity and increase yeast activity by providing more sucrose for the yeast. The sweet starter maintains more gluten structure in the dough, which enables sourdough bakers to make some of the more challenging doughs that need gluten structure; things like donuts, pastries and brioche. For these enriched, laminated doughs you will need to refresh the sourdough starter three times using the sweet refreshment guide in the 36 hours before starting your bake, adding 25g of sugar each time. The addition of sugar retards fermentation by osmosis. This draws water away from the yeast cells and slows down the fermentation. Adding sugar to the starter encourages the osmotolerant yeast to multiply. This means that the yeasts that cope with extra sugar increase in population, resulting in a good rise in the laminated doughs, and a beautiful open crumb.

In the sweet starter, the acid level must be carefully managed. This allows the enzyme (amylase) to break down the starch into simple sugars that feed the yeast. Certain strains of yeast, in particular *S. cerevisiae*, don't like to be in an environment that's too acidic. You need very high levels of yeast to leaven enriched doughs. Your ideal temperature for this starter to ferment at is between 22–26°C. It doesn't look any different to the sour one, but it will make a significant difference to the structure of your dough.

You can easily switch between the two refreshments to create either a sour or sweet starter. Note this is a very thick starter. The thickness encourages oxygen, which increases yeast. The timings given right and overleaf are designed to fit this in around a normal working day, but you can adjust by one or two hours if your schedule is different.

30G STARTER

ADD 60G WATER

ADD 100G FLOUR

**FOR EACH REFRESHMENT
OF THE SOUR WHOLEGRAIN STARTER**

30g (about 1 tablespoon) starter (page 106)
60g water at 16–18°C (61–64°F)
100g stoneground wholegrain flour or
    Botanical Blend no.2

**FOR EACH REFRESHMENT
OF THE SWEET WHOLEGRAIN STARTER**

30g (about 1 tablespoon) starter (from page 106)
    or from a previously established starter
60g water at 16–18°C (61–64°F)
100g stoneground wholegrain flour or
    Botanical Blend no.2
25g sugar

*You will need two similarly sized pots with lids
(see Tip on page 110)*

# First build

**Day 1—9pm**

Put your 30g starter in a pot. Add the water, then add the flour (and sugar, if you're making the sweet starter).

Stir vigorously to combine the ingredients and oxygenate the water; yeasts need some oxygen to reproduce.

Put the lid onto the pot, taking care not to make it airtight or you risk an explosion when the gases build up during fermentation. Leave the pot on the kitchen worksurface at an ambient temperature of about 20–22oC (68–72°F) (an average temperature in a kitchen).

# Second build

**Day 2—8am**

Take 30g of the starter and refresh it again following the steps above; it is what we call a "double refresh" or "back to back" refreshment and really builds up the microbes before you start to bake. See chart on page 114.

STIR

COVER AND LEAVE IN WARM PLACE

AFTER 5-8 HOURS

## Mix and/or third build

**Day 2**—When the starter has peaked (is at its highest point in the pot) you can do the following.

**8pm**—you can use it to mix one of the non-advanced recipes (pages 122–167).

Then you could either put the sourdough starter in the fridge until next needed, or:

**9pm**—refresh a third time, as a final build that absolutely ensures successful results from an advanced bake or sourdough boule.

Obviously, it is not compulsory to make a non-advanced bake as you build, but at the School we never miss an opportunity to bake, and someone always appreciates a bake!

Please see page 109 for a detailed schedule showing exactly when to complete each stage of this process.

Tip I use two pots because it allows me to soak and clean one while the other is in use or keep two starters on the go, with one as a back-up or ready to use for other recipes.

### HOW LONG CAN I STORE MY STARTER FOR?

It's a tricky question, but for every week you leave your starter, refresh it twice (a double refreshment). Try not to leave your starter longer than a week, but if you do, simply rebuild it by refreshing it continually, back to back without a fridge break, until it doubles in size with ease in about 5–6 hours. If it's not responding, give it rye.

# Why do you need a leaven?

You generally only need a leaven for an advanced retarded bake. A leaven is a young, newly refreshed sourdough starter used to make dough rise. So, the advanced recipes (pages 168–182) call for a leaven. A leaven basically controls the rate of fermentation to achieve an optimally risen bake. Leavens are often overlooked by bakers. While the starter is the foundation of your bake, a leaven also offers one of the very best opportunities to increase your Diversity score by using different Botanical blends.

The simplest way to think of a leaven is as a young inoculant. An old inoculant (such as a fully mature starter) will acidify the gluten too much and will break down the structure before it has finished proving.

In this book, we've only used the leavens for the advanced bakes. These are mostly the retarded techniques. The formula and timings for the leaven is included in each recipe. It's very simple: you're essentially stirring your microbially active, superstar, triple-refreshed, Olympic athlete starter in with some more flour and water to ensure a fantastically Instagram-able, well-risen bake with a beautiful crumb structure (for a full explanation, refer to the chart on page 114).

### WHY DO YOU MAKE LEAVENS WITH DIFFERENT KINDS OF FLOUR AND DIFFERENT WATER TEMPERATURES?

Leavens give you control over the level of inoculation and therefore the rate of fermentation. Wholegrain, warm leavens can be used quite quickly, whereas cooler, white roller-milled flour leavens ferment more slowly and so will take longer to be ready to use: possibly even overnight. You use the leaven most appropriate to your timing to allow you to get on with real life.
**Right, Botanical blend no.3. Most leavens are ready between 2-4 hours old, depending on the ambient temperature and the kind of flour you are using.**

## Notes

..................................................

..................................................

..................................................

..................................................

..................................................

..................................................

..................................................

..................................................

..................................................

..................................................

..................................................

..................................................

..................................................

..................................................

## Other important factors to consider

**AMBIENT TEMPERATURE**
It's important to consider the ambient temperature of your kitchen. Here at the School, it is about 22°C (72°F) in the bakery most of the year, so we adjust the temperature of our leavens by 2–3°C one way or another depending on how hot or cold the room is.

Likewise, if you are in a colder climate, you might want to move your leaven to a warmer spot. If you are in a warmer climate, consider starting with colder water.

## The rhythm of baking

Many of my students hate throwing sourdough starter away. On page 114, you will find a chart: "Understanding your starter and how refreshing it works". This clearly lays out the whole process, including what can be done with the "discard" of each level of build. Baking sweet sourdough minimizes your discard. Incorporating these bakes becomes part of the rhythm of building your starter's microbial activity high enough to successfully bake an advanced bake or boule.

The crumb structure
of the Miso prune Danish
(see page 175)

# Understanding your starter and how refreshing it works

As a domestic baker you need to plan ahead. In a bakery there is no need to do this, because you use your starter every single day and it is always microbially active. At home, it is a different matter. You need to rebuild the number of microbes and use it at the most appropriate time to get the results you want. You might find it helpful to imagine your starter as growing younger with each refreshment. Every time you refresh it, the starter gets a new lease of life and grows stronger and more powerful, and so the things you can use it for change according to what "age" it is at in its lifecycle.

## FIRST BUILD

### Relative age: 90

After a week in the fridge your starter is little, old and tired. (If your starter has been in the fridge for just 24–48 hours you, might find that it is still microbially active enough after just 1 refreshment to go straight to the 3rd build).

### What to do with it

Refresh. Use the discard from the bottom of the pot for Porridge pots (page 122) or in the Russian rye recipe on page 127 of my book *The Sourdough School*.

## SECOND BUILD

### Relative age: 40

The second build has given your starter a whole new lease of life. It might not be at its absolute bread-making prime, but it's going to be perfect for the cakes, biscuits, pastries and tin bakes in this book. We want the proteolytic enzyme activity to break down the gluten to make the bake more digestible.

### What to do with it

Refresh if you want to progress. Use this starter (or the discard, if you're progressing) for cakes, traybakes and biscuits.

## THIRD BUILD

### Relative age: 18

Not only is this third build a sprightly, lively 18-year-old, it's also the bread-making equivalent of an Olympic athlete. It's strong, robust and in the prime of life.

This starter is at its absolute microbial peak, with the highest possible microbial cell density for leavening power and flavor.

It is a good idea to build before storage: if you need to stop baking for a few days, you need to maintain the highest numbers possible in the fridge ready for next time you bake.

### What to do with it

Because of the lengthy fermentation process of sourdough bread, your dough will "age" by about 80 years during fermentation. You don't want to bake with a 98-year-old, so to control the lifecycle you will need to make a leaven.

## LEAVEN

### Relative age: 2

This is a crazy toddler, full of life. It is young and sweet with low levels of acidity, which means that the amylase enzymes are able to best break down the starch in the flour into simple sugars to feed the yeast and bacteria (pH levels of 6.7–7 are optimal for amylase). It also reduces the proteolytic enzyme activity so it doesn't break down too much gluten protein, meaning the bake retains a good structure. (Proteolytic enzymes like a lower acidity, of about pH 4–5). See page 104.

During the fermentation process, the leaven will age as part of the lifecycle of making retarded bread, cakes or pastries. So, after a long, cold prove, and by the time you're ready to bake, it will be a sprightly 80-year-old. This is so important, because once it's in the oven, it needs a bit of life left in it to get its final lease of life (known as "oven spring") and so in its final moments of life in the heat of the oven it has enough energy to go out in glory which gives you a wonderful, open, well-risen bake. Think of your dough still having the energy for one last dance.

### What to do with it

A young leaven is used for advanced retarded bakes such as boule and all of the advanced recipes on pages 168–182. It is used to delay the acidification (see enzymes page 104), which allows gluten development as you mix the dough and therefore develops the structure of the bake early on before it begins to break down. This only really matters when the fermentation is long and slow.

# Schedule for non-advanced bakes

| | |
|---|---|
| **Thursday pm** | Refresh starter (first build). |
| **Friday am** | Refresh starter (second build). |
| **Friday pm** | Mix dough and prove ambiently overnight. Return your starter to the fridge until the next bake. |
| **Saturday am** | Bake. |

Note With repeat refreshing, you are always going to end up with a discard. The cost of discard at the current rate of cost of the most basic bread flour you can buy in the UK ranges from 2 to 8 pence per 100g. There are many other ways of using up this discard, including using it in non-sourdough recipes such as pancakes and waffles. I advise always keeping a separate jar in the fridge so you can use up your discard in all of these different ways. One of my favorite recipes is the Russian Rye recipe on page 127 of *The Sourdough School* book.

# Schedule for advanced bakes and retarded sourdough bread

**THE VERY BEST WAYS EVER TO USE UP THE DISCARD FROM BUILDING A STARTER**
I'll let you into a secret—I only really bake the non-advanced cakes as I am building my starters to bake retarded sourdough boules (see my last book *The Sourdough School*), or as I build my starter for an advanced bake. You see, baking sourdough cakes is actually one of the very best ways to use up the discard from building your starter. So, this is my rough guide to scheduling advanced bakes and baking retarded sourdough bread:

| | |
|---|---|
| **Thursday pm** | Refresh starter (first build). |
| **Friday am** | Refresh starter (second build). You can use the discard to make a sweet bake/cake and leave the cake to prove during the day (you will need to inverse the suggested timings, mix the cake in the morning and ferment all day, and bake in the evening). |
| **Friday pm** | Refresh starter (third build). Bake the cake. Again, you can use the discard to make a sweet bake/cake and leave the cake to prove overnight. |
| **Saturday am** | Make your leaven (fourth build). Remember to return your starter to the fridge. Bake the cake, leaving your leaven to prove while you bake. Use the leaven (now 2–3 hours old) to make an advanced bake such as donuts and/or retarded bread dough. Prove your dough (ambiently) during the day. Retard your dough overnight in the fridge. |
| **Sunday am** | Take your dough out of the fridge early and prepare. Bake your bread. |
| **Sunday pm** | Prove advanced sweet bakes for most of the day. Bake late afternoon. |

# Notes

# The recipes

# Essential baking advice

Before you start baking, here are some last bits of baking advice and troubleshooting tips to bear in mind throughout this chapter. Please read this before you start baking, or you'll learn it the hard way!

## Hydration

You will need to slightly adjust the hydration in every bake. An element of judgement is required for the thickness of the batter and making minor adjustments, as needed. I appreciate that if you are a beginner, this might seem a little bit daunting, but the batter needs to fall off the spoon willingly when you hold it above the bowl. I encourage students at the School to connect to the way the mixture feels. What seems like a very small amount of water actually has a major effect on the openness and lightness of the crumb structure.

### MY MIXTURE IS TOO DRY

In exactly the same way as you bassinage bread, you can add extra water in increments of 10g at a time to adjustment the hydration. Mix this in incrementally over about 10–15 minutes. Giving the flour time to absorb the water is actually how you find the optimal hydration level for that particular blend. I can't emphasize enough how important this is: it is the difference between an open, light bake and a heavy, closed one. It's also the main opportunity to connect to your dough, and part of the mindfulness of baking is in adding the water and mixing with your hands.

### MY MIXTURE IS TOO SLOPPY

It's very difficult to know exactly how much bran or protein is in your flour or blend. I always wait 10 minutes before making an adjustment, especially when using freshly milled flour, because it sometimes takes longer to fully hydrate. At that point, you can sift and hand mix in about 10g flour, then wait another 10 minutes.

## Digestion

If you suspect that you have a gluten intolerance, it is absolutely essential that you see your GP. If your GP gives you the all-clear health-wise, one of the most powerful aids to your digestion is to leave your dough to ferment longer. You can increase the breakdown by putting the dough in the fridge, covered, at the end of the fermentation process. This will extend the fermentation for another 6–8 hours in the fridge before baking. The breakdown of the gluten through the protease activity during fermentation significantly reduces the gluten load. It does not, however, remove all gluten. As a secondary measure we have, wherever possible, used heritage grains throughout the blends in this book. While they do still contain gluten, the make-up of the gluten and the structure of the proteins are different and there is some evidence to suggest less inflammatory responses from gluten in heritage grains.

If you suffer with IBS or other digestive issues, you might begin by using the Hybrid blend (Botanical blend no. 1, page 55), as it contains a little less fibre, and reduces the ratio of wholegrain flour right down to 10 per cent. You can then slowly increase the amount of wholegrain you use, little by little each week. One of the key things about increasing fibre in your diet, even fermented fibre, is taking it a little bit at a time. I understand it's life-changing to be able to enjoy eating cakes and bakes again, however my advice is to give yourself time to adjust to minimize digestive discomfort. It can be overwhelming for your digestive system by going from 0–10 in one go.

# How to get the DDT

DDT is a phrase you'll see throughout the recipe chapter. It stands for Desired Dough Temperature. Getting it right takes time and practice. If you store your ingredients somewhere cold, you can take them out and bring them to room temperature before mixing. If you store them somewhere warm, pop them in the fridge to cool a little before you bake. Try to mix the flour and liquid to get the DDT as close as possible to the one recommended in the book. It's worth the effort; achieving the correct dough temperature is crucial to a successful bake. The DDT is a major factor in following the timings suggested in this book. If you need to alter your timings, you can lower or raise your DDT by 2–3°C (36–37°F) to speed things up or slow things down. It takes practice to find the optimal timings and DDT for your kitchen and flour blend.

# My bake is too sour

You can decrease sourness by baking it an hour or two earlier or lowering the DDT by 2–3°C (36–37°F).

# Shortcuts

Any of the following shortcuts can save you time.

### SHOP-BOUGHT INSTEAD OF HOMEMADE
▶ Organic syrups made with raw cane sugar are available from most good health food shops and can be used instead of the homemade ones on pages 84–89.
▶ Most supermarkets now stock organic kefir that actually contain the probiotics listed on pages 62–68. Please look at the label. Of course, you can use one of these to start your own kefir.
▶ You can buy frozen fruit to make compotes (page 83), or even buy ready-made compotes if you don't have fruit in season.

### IF YOU DON'T HAVE A MILL
▶ You can still bake from this book without a mill. Simply buy 3–4 bags of different heritage flours and mix them up. Consider adding a tablespoon of unsweetened chocolate powder or flax seeds, or have a look for some interesting prebiotic powders you can stir in. Play!
▶ You can buy many ingredients ready-milled, such as flax seeds.

# Bugs in grain

Organic grains have organic bugs. If you leave your grain long enough, they will hatch. At the School, we always freeze our grain for 48 hours before use to kill any microscopic eggs. I'd rather do this than eat pesticides.

# Advice on using flour

Whether it is a Botanical blend or a wholegrain flour, it's your main ingredient, and flour differs depending on many factors. It can be frustrating when you first start baking, because trying to get exactly the same results with a different flour can be challenging. Older flour can absorb more water, as can flour that is higher in protein or fibre. Some heritage grains are much lower in gluten and can ferment faster. It takes time to identify and become familiar with the flour you use and sometimes it can take me 2–3 bakes to really find the right levels of hydration and precise timings for each flour or blend that we create.

Blackberry & cultured cream mini cakes (page 148). Beautifully fermented and easily digested.

# Chocolate & raspberry porridge breakfast pots

**THE GUT FACTOR** THIS PROVIDES MULTIPLE PREBIOTIC SUBSTRATES TO NOURISH A WIDE RANGE OF MICROBES, WITH PROBIOTIC SUPPORT TO THE GUT FROM THE LIVE YOGURT AND YOUR STARTER, AS WELL AS HIGH LEVELS OF POLYPHENOLS FROM THE BERRIES. **SUGGESTED BOTANICAL BLEND** ANY DIVERSITY MUESLI MIX **PROBIOTIC** YOGURT

▶ **STARTER** SOUR

▶ **INGREDIENTS**

100g Diversity muesli mix (page 58)

about 300g water (see method), plus an additional 10–20g if needed

30g starter (first build discard, refreshed about 1 week previously; page 114; see schedule, or use kefir in place of starter)

10g salted butter or coconut oil

100g live Yogurt (page 72)

100g Fresh fruit compote (page 83) or raspberry jello

12g bittersweet chocolate

10g chopped pistachios

small punnet of fresh raspberries (about 300g)

*You will need 3–4 sterilized jam jars*

▶ **DDT** 23°C (73°F)

▶ **SCHEDULE**

Day 1  6pm   **Make porridge and leave to cool and thicken**

       9pm   **Add the starter and divide into pots. Ferment overnight**

Day 2  7.30am **Ready to eat**

Tip **It is difficult to give you a precise measurement for how much water you will need, because every grain, seed and fruit in the muesli mix will hydrate slightly differently. The mixture needs to look slightly more liquid than you think it should, because it will continue to absorb water and thicken as the porridge cools. Because of this, make the porridge 3–4 hours ahead of time.**

The overnight fermentation of these breakfast pots essentially acts as external digestion, and the acids that the bacteria create make it easier for your gut microbes to access the fibre and nutrients, making the porridge more nutritious and easier to digest. Be sure to make the porridge in advance so that it has time to cool and absorb the water (see Tip). Taste a tiny bit of your starter before you use it, to ensure it is sour. The sourness is an indicator of acidity, which ensures that only the positive microbes that we want to culture in your starter are present. Higher levels of acidity are a deterrent to pathogenic bacteria.

Put the Diversity muesli mix into a saucepan with 200–250g of the water and the butter or coconut oil, and place over a low heat. Stir, making sure that, as the water is absorbed and the porridge begins to thicken, it doesn't catch on the bottom. As it thickens, add more water incrementally (see Tip) and keep stirring until the porridge is thoroughly cooked, which will take a good 8–10 minutes.

Leave the porridge to cool and continue thickening for about 3 hours. Once it has cooled to about 23°C (73°F), you can stir in your starter. Take the starter from the bottom of the pot: it will look like heavy cream.

Divide equally into 3–4 sterilized jam jars, cover with a clean, damp dish towel, and leave to ferment overnight on the kitchen worksurface.

By the morning, the porridge will have fermented and risen slightly in the jar. Add the yogurt and fruit compote or jello, then top each jar with chopped chocolate, pistachios and fresh raspberries. Eat at room temperature.

These breakfast pots are ideal for a busy family, but remember that live food is still fermenting, especially when it is warm, so there will be build-up of carbon dioxide which can crack sealed jars. So, if you don't want to eat your pot straight away, remember to pop it in the fridge after its overnight fermentation. It will keep for up to 2 days.

# Farinata

**THE GUT FACTOR** CONTAINS NOURISHING *AKKERMANSIA*, A STRATEGY TO CROWD OUT THE PATHOGENIC BACTERIA AND STRENGTHEN EPITHELIAL LAYERS.
**SUGGESTED BOTANICAL BLEND** NO. 10: BEANS
**PROBIOTIC** YOGURT

Garbanzos are high in raffinose oligosaccharides and can positively influence your gut microbiome. A study on mice showed that eating a diet high in garbanzos strengthened the epithelial layers of the intestine. Another study on humans in 2009 by University of Saskatchewan showed a reduction in pathological bacteria to the point that the "garbanzos and raffinose have the potential to modulate the intestinal microbial composition [and] promote intestinal health in humans".

Pomegranates were the food of Greek gods, and are are thought to be fruit that tempted Adam. They are mostly composed of water and a little pectin (page 27), which is a prebiotic dietary fibre, but they are also rich in polyphenols like flavonoids (page 29), anthocyanins (page 30), and ellagitannins, which are known to protect the body's cells and DNA from oxidative stress. In particular, ellagitannins have been shown in animal studies to increase levels of *Akkermansia*, a microbe whose activities can strengthen the lining of the gut.

▶ **STARTER** SWEET OR SOUR

▶ **FOR THE "PANCAKES"**
200g garbanzo flour or Botanical blend no. 10 (page 57)
4g salt
15g bubbly, lively starter or discard (page 114; see schedule)
350g water, plus an additional 10–20g if needed
90g Auntie's ghee (page 79), for greasing

▶ **TO SERVE**
1 pomegranate
pomegranate syrup, to drizzle
live yogurt (page 72)

▶ **DDT** 20°C (68°F)

▶ **SCHEDULE**
Day 1  9pm  Refresh starter (first build)
Day 2  8am  Refresh starter (second build)
       8pm  Mix batter and return the starter to the fridge (unless you are proceeding to a third build). Prepare your yogurt. Prove/ferment overnight
Day 3  8am  Bake

## Tip
Don't be tempted to fry this—it doesn't have the stability to be flipped.

Mix together the flour, salt and starter in a bowl, making sure it is at the DDT. Add the water to create a runny batter.

Ferment overnight, covered, on the kitchen worksurface.

The next morning, preheat the oven to its maximum temperature. Once it's hot, grease a large, 30cm (12-inch) ovenproof frying skillet with about 30g of the ghee. Place the greased pan in the oven to preheat. The hot ghee will create a seal between the pan and the batter.

Remove the pan from the oven when the ghee is almost at smoking point. Be careful and use oven gloves, as it will be very hot. Add about a third of the batter to the pan and gently tilt the pan from side to side so that the batter covers the surface. Immediately bake for 2–3 minutes until golden.

Repeat with the remaining ghee and batter. Serve the farinata with fresh pomegranate seeds, a generous drizzle of pomegranate syrup and a spoonful of live yogurt.

# Mulberry galette

**THE GUT FACTOR** MULBERRIES ARE HIGH IN
THE PHENOLIC COMPOUNDS.
**SUGGESTED BOTANICAL BLEND** NO. 3: RED
**PROBIOTIC** CULTURED CREAM

▶ **STARTER** SWEET OR SOUR

▶ **INGREDIENTS**

300g Botanical blend no. 3 (page 56) or
    stoneground, wholegrain flour
150g sweet butter, plus extra for
    greasing
4g sea salt
30g coconut sugar
60g bubbly, lively starter or discard (page 114;
    see schedule)
1 egg yolk
30g ground almonds
½ teaspoon vanilla powder
300g mulberries (or other dark berries; see intro)

▶ **TO SERVE**

20g runny honey
20g melted sweet butter
Cultured cream (page 72), to serve

▶ **DDT** 22°C (72°F)

▶ **SCHEDULE**

Day 1  9pm    Refresh starter (first build)
Day 2  8am    Refresh starter (second build)
       6pm    Mix dough and return the starter to
              the fridge (unless you are proceeding
              to a third build). Prepare your Cultured
              cream. Leave to prove/ferment
Day 3  9am    Push dough into tin to create pastry
              base. Chill until needed
              When ready, top the pastry and bake

You could use spelt to make this simple galette, or any stoneground, wholegrain flour, but the combination of hibiscus and roses in Botanical blend no. 3 enhances both the levels of nutrients and the flavors. Mulberries are high in the phenolic compounds that many studies suggest play a critical role in the health of the intestinal microbiome. They have been used in Chinese medicine for thousands of years for treating sore throats, anemia, and tonsillitis. There are over 20 species of mulberry and more than 1,000 cultivars, predominately originating in south-east Asian countries, including red (*M. rubra L.*), black (*M. nigra L.*), and white (*M. alba L*). The darker varieties have higher levels of polyphenols.

Dark fruits such as blackberries, raspberries, cherries or blackcurrants work beautifully with hibiscus, which has been used as a herbal medicine in many cultures due to its antibacterial, antioxidant, anti-cholesterol and diuretic properties, as well as its anti-diabetic and anti-hypertensive actions. In a study on obese mice, hibiscus was able to reduce the ratio of *Firmicutes* to *Bacteroidetes* (a high ratio is associated with obesity) and also modify the abundance of different genera while reducing inflammation markers.

In a bowl, mix together the flour and butter to form breadcrumbs. Add the salt and sugar. The mixture should be quite dry. Now add the starter and the egg yolk to bring the pastry together. It needs to be able to form a ball and feel "together" but not wet. It should be a cross between a biscuit and shortbread texture. It will break down further as it ferments.

Cover the bowl and leave on the side to ferment overnight.

The next day, preheat the oven to 170°C/340°F/Gas Mark 3½ and grease and line a 24cm (9½-inch) tart tin with greased baking parchment. Use your fingers to push the pastry into the lined tin.

In a small bowl, mix together the ground almonds and vanilla powder, then sprinkle over the base. Arrange the mulberries on top of the pastry and drizzle over the honey and melted butter.

Bake for 25–30 minutes. Once cooled, serve with Cultured cream (page 72).

# Diversity pikelets

**THE GUT FACTOR** GREAT DIVERSITY AND RICH IN FIBRE,
PROBIOTICS AND POLYPHENOLS.
**SUGGESTED BOTANICAL BLEND** YOUR CHOICE OF BLENDS NO. 3–9
**PROBIOTIC** CULTURED CREAM

A pikelet is a cross between a scone and a crumpet, but it is thinner and has more freedom in shape. Pikelets are quick to make and, because of the lactic acid produced during fermentation, have increased levels of resistant starch that nourishes gut microbes and helps to keep blood sugars stable. The acidity also means that they remain fresh for longer. We always serve these with a pot of Fresh fruit compote made with berries, as dark fruits are loaded with polyphenols. Cultured cream is full of beneficial live bacteria, which is the perfect excuse for me to encourage my students to indulge in a very generous helping.

▶ **STARTER** SWEET OR SOUR

▶ **INGREDIENTS**
150g bubbly, lively starter or discard (page 114; see schedule)
250g buttermilk (you can use kefir if you don't have buttermilk)
2 tablespoons fresh lemon juice
250g white or sifted spelt flour
200g your chosen Botanical blend (pages 55–57) or stoneground, wholegrain flour
150g slightly salted butter, chilled, cut in small pieces
½ teaspoon sea salt
75g coconut sugar
oil, for greasing
1 egg, beaten with 1 tablespoon of milk, for the glaze

▶ **TO SERVE**
Cultured cream (page 72)
Fresh fruit compote (page 83)

▶ **DDT** 20°C (68°F)

▶ **SCHEDULE**
Day 1  9pm    Refresh starter (first build)
Day 2  8am    Refresh starter (second build)
       8pm    Mix dough and return the starter to the fridge (unless you are proceeding to a third build). Prepare your Cultured cream. Prove/ferment overnight
Day 3  8am    Cut out the pikelets and leave to rest
       10am   Bake (or place in the fridge until you're ready to bake)

In a large measuring jug, whisk together the starter, buttermilk and lemon juice, then set aside.

Put the flours, butter and salt into a bowl and rub the butter into the flour until you have a mixture that resembles breadcrumbs. Add the sugar and stir to combine.

Make a well in the centre of the flour mixture and pour in the starter mixture. Bring the mixture together to form a rough dough. If the dough seems a bit dry, add a little water; just a few drops until the mixture comes together. On the other hand, if it's too sticky to handle easily, add a small amount of flour.

Form the dough into a ball, oil the bowl, and return the ball to the bowl. Cover the bowl with a damp dish towel and leave on the kitchen worksurface to prove overnight.

The following morning, oil the table, and lightly grease two baking trays. Press the dough out lightly on table to form a rectangle about 30 x 20cm (12 x 8 inches). Use a 8cm (3¼-inch) cutter to cut the dough into 14–16 pikelets. Place the pikelets on the prepared trays. Cover and leave on the kitchen worksurface for 2 hours to "come back to life".

Preheat your oven to 180°C/350°F/Gas Mark 4. Brush the pikelets with the egg wash. Bake for 10–12 minutes until golden. Cool on a wire rack. Serve with Cultured cream and Fresh fruit compote.

# Honey, orange & dukkha sweet pappardelle

**THE GUT FACTOR** CONTAINS SELENIUM
**SUGGESTED BOTANICAL BLEND** NO. 8: ORIENTAL
**PROBIOTIC** CULTURED BUTTER

▶ **STARTER** SWEET OR SOUR

▶ **FOR THE PASTA DOUGH**
100g Botanical blend no. 8 (page 57) or
   Khorasan flour
50g wholemeal spelt
50g "00" flour
2g salt
4 large egg yolks, at room temperature
50g bubbly, lively starter or discard (page 114;
   see schedule)
olive oil, for oiling
about 20g water, if needed
1 tablespoon chestnut flour or rice flour,
   to prevent sticking

▶ **TO FINISH**
20g Cultured butter (page 79)
2 tablespoons dark runny honey
juice from 1 Seville orange, lemon or lime
35g Dukkha (see page 146)

*You will need a pasta machine*

▶ **DDT** 20°C (68°F)

▶ **SCHEDULE**

| Day 1 | 9pm | Refresh starter (first build) |
|---|---|---|
| Day 2 | 8am | Refresh starter (second build) |
| | 9pm | Mix dough and return the starter to the fridge (unless you are proceeding to a third build) |
| Day 3 | Midday | Roll out dough and cut, then cook on the same day |

Pasta as a pudding! This is an incredibly simple dish that, once the dough is ready, can be created in minutes. The key is getting the right combination of sweetness, nuttiness and a little tartness from the citrus. Khorasan, used in blend no. 8, is a durum-based flour. It's buttery and yellow and full of selenium. Some initial studies on mice indicate that selenium may protect the intestinal barrier against potential pathogens, and epidemiological studies have found a significant link between a higher selenium status and a lower risk of colorectal cancer. Khorasan is also high in protein (normally 16 per cent). I love using it to make this pasta, but if you like you can use the same technique and vary the flour. Senatore Cappelli, an Italian wheat flour, or any durum wheat would be fabulous here. Orange is an aromatic proven to improve mood, and the perfect accompaniment.

Mix the flours and salt together in a bowl, then pour them onto your worksurface in a heap. Form a well in the centre, then add the egg yolks and sourdough starter. Using a fork or your fingers, gradually incorporate the liquid into the dry ingredients. This is going to be a dry dough. It will feel tight and take some effort to bring together. If you really feel you can't get it to come together, dip your hand into some water and knead the mixture again with the extra liquid. I can't tell you exactly how much water you might need to add (see Tips overleaf), but you are looking to finish with a butter-yellow, smooth textured dough.

Once there is no dry flour remaining, start kneading. Because this is a dry dough it is going to take some work, but you need to develop the gluten structure before it ferments. You want to create a pliable, malleable dough. Again, add a little water if you really need to, just a few drops at a time, but take care not to add too much.

Place the dough in a lightly oiled bowl, cover and leave on the kitchen worksurface to ferment.

## Variation

Replace the honey with maple syrup and the dukkha with toasted walnuts for a different flavor combination.

..................................................

## Tips

Khorasan can be very thirsty, so you may need to adjust the hydration slightly depending on the age, fibre content, protein content and fineness of the flour.

Due to the proteolytic action (gluten degredation) of the sourdough this pasta does not keep and must be eaten on the same day.

When you are ready to cook the pasta, oil your worksurface with a few drops of olive oil. (I prefer to use oil rather than flour because I don't want to introduce excess flour at this stage and end up eating it raw).

Roll the dough out until you have a thin sheet measuring about 28 x 24cm (11 x 9½ inches). Fold the dough in half lengthways, making it 14 x 24cm (5½ x 9½ inches) so it fits through your pasta machine. Pass it through the pasta machine again. Repeat this process three times to strengthen the gluten.

Cut the pasta sheet into four strips, then roll each strip through the pasta machine until the machine is on a middle setting (don't go too thin, or it will fall apart). Cut the pasta into pappardelle, with a width of about 2.5cm (1 inch), using a sharp knife. Dust your fresh pasta with a little chestnut or rice flour. Leave to relax for 10–15 minutes, during which time you can bring a pot of water to the boil. If you prefer you can leave it in the fridge for 4–6 hours. When ready, drop the pasta straight into a large saucepan of boiling water. Cook for about 3½ minutes; I like it al dente. It cooks very quickly, so don't leave it too long.

Drain the pasta, then return it to the warm pan and toss with a generous knob of cultured butter, the honey, citrus juice and dukkha (page 146). Reserve a little of the dukkha to garnish. Eat and enjoy immediately.

# Tortas de aceite

**THE GUT FACTOR** FIBRE IS THE FUEL THAT OUR GUT MICROBES NEED TO MAKE SHORT CHAIN FATTY ACIDS THAT ARE THE MAIN SOURCE OF ENERGY FOR THE CELLS LINING YOUR COLON.
**SUGGESTED BOTANICAL BLEND** NOS. 7, 8 OR 9
**PROBIOTIC** SERVE WITH SOURDOUGH FIZZ

These moreish Spanish olive oil biscuits are modelled on ones I bought from Spain. They are delicious, but the commercial version is high in sugar and low in fibre. I use white stoneground flour that retains a considerable amount of fibre: 4.5g per 100g. The flax seeds contain 27g fibre per 100g. In total, your microbes are getting 15 times the amount of fibre provided by the commercial versions. You can increase the diversity score by adding sesame seeds, aniseed seeds, dill seeds or lemon zest. You can also use grated jaggery or honey instead of coconut sugar.

▶ **STARTER** SWEET OR SOUR

▶ **FOR THE DOUGH**
100g bubbly, lively starter or discard (page 114; see schedule)
250g white spelt or stoneground, flour, sieved
5g salt
75g olive oil
1 tablespoon aniseeds, sesame seeds, fennel seeds, or dill seeds (avoid adding seeds if you if you suffer from IBS)
1 tablespoon orange zest
½ teaspoon vanilla powder
35g golden flax seeds
100g water, plus an additional 10–20g if needed

▶ **TO FINISH**
100g olive oil
5 tablespoons coconut sugar or to taste

▶ **DDT** 24°C (75°F)

▶ **SCHEDULE**
Day 1  9pm    Refresh starter (first build)
Day 2  8am    Refresh starter (second build)
       8pm    Mix dough and return the starter to the fridge (unless you are proceeding to a third build). Prove overnight
Day 3  9am    Divide dough
       10am   Roll out
       12.30pm Bake

Tip It's difficult to fully avoid the sugar in this recipe because the topping is caramelized, but I've drastically reduced the quantity and included vanilla and a pinch of sea salt to increase natural sweetness.

In a large bowl, mix together all the dough ingredients except the water, including the seeds and orange zest. Add the water gradually—you may need adjust the hydration, depending on how much bran is in your wholegrain flour. Cover the bowl and leave to prove at an ambient temperature overnight.

When the dough has risen, divide it into 12 balls. Cover and leave them for another hour to rest. Preheat the oven to 200°C/400°F/Gas Mark 6 and line a baking tray with baking parchment.

Roll each of the balls out on a worksurface. Each one should create a circle, 12–15cm (4½–6 inches) in diameter. Transfer each biscuit to the prepared baking tray. Now glug the olive oil over the top of the biscuits. It looks like a lot, but leave for 3–4 minutes and you'll see the biscuits absorb it. Sprinkle coconut sugar over each biscuit.

Bake for about 8–10 minutes. Keep a close eye on them after 7 minutes. You want the biscuits to crisp and the sugar to caramelize, but not to burn. Take the tray out of the oven. Be careful—the oil and sugar will be extremely hot. Leave to cool. If you think that they're not dry enough, pop them back into the cooling oven with the door open, but ensure they don't bake further. Leave them to absorb the oil for a few more minutes. Transfer them to a wire rack.

Store the cooled biscuits in greaseproof paper in an airtight container. I think they are at their best on day 3. Serve with a glass of Sourdough fizz (page 92). The dough can also be kept in the fridge for about 3 days and baked when needed. It will become more sour and broken down each day.

# Morello cherry shortbread

**THE GUT FACTOR** CONTAINS NOURISHING *AKKERMANSIA*, MICROBES THAT HELP STRENGTHEN THE GUT LINING.
**SUGGESTED BOTANICAL BLEND** NO. 3 (RED BLEND)
**PROBIOTIC** SERVE WITH CHERRY AND EARL GREY KVASS

▶ **STARTER** SWEET OR SOUR

▶ **INGREDIENTS**

500g stoneground wholegrain flour

10g salt

100g bubbly, lively starter or discard (page 114; see schedule)

150g coconut sugar

175g crunchy peanut butter

250g unsalted butter, plus extra for greasing

70g Morello cherries (if using frozen be sure to drain them), or other dark fruit

30g Dukkha (see page 146)

1 egg, beaten with 1 tablespoon of milk or watered down kefir, for the eggwash

▶ **TO FINISH**

2 tablespoons Cherry syrup (see page 87)

▶ **DDT** 22°C (72°F)

▶ **SCHEDULE**

| | | |
|---|---|---|
| Day 1 | 9pm | Refresh starter (first build) |
| Day 2 | 8am | Refresh starter (second build) |
| | 8pm | Mix dough and return the starter to the fridge (unless you are proceeding to a third build). Wrap the dough in greaseproof paper and prove overnight |
| Day 3 | 8am | Transfer dough to fridge to set |
| Day 3 | | When you're ready, slice the dough and bake |

Sensual, dark and sweet, cherries are opulence and luxury incarnate. They are a rich source of polyphenols (page 29), which help reduce oxidative stress on the body's cells and prevent inflammation, two processes that are linked to mood disorders and chronic diseases. They also contain melatonin, vitamin C, fibre and carotenoids. An early study in mice suggests that dark, sweet cherries may enhance beneficial SCFA production by gut microbes and increase levels of *Akkermansia*, microbes that help strengthen the gut lining.

I serve these shortbreads with my Cherry and Earl Grey kvass (page 95), as a different take on tea and biscuits. These biscuits are both sweet and sour, moreish and satiating. They are soft, crunchy, crumbly and salty. This is a bake-as-you need recipe. The dough will keep in the fridge for up to 1 week.

In a large bowl, mix together the flour, starter, sugar, peanut butter, butter and cherries. Shape the dough into a log.

Take a piece of greaseproof paper and grease it with butter. Generously sprinkle over the dukkha. Place the dough log on the greaseproof paper and roll in dukkha to evenly cover. Roll it up like a Christmas cracker, pinching the ends, and leave it aside overnight to ferment on the worksurface.

The following morning, place the wrapped dough in the fridge to set and preheat the oven to 160°C/325°F/Gas Mark 3. Lightly grease a baking tray.

Remove the dough from the fridge when needed, and use a serrated knife to slice it into 20 7–10mm (½-inch) rounds. Place on the prepared baking tray, lightly brush with egg wash and bake for 18–20 minutes, until golden.

Remove from the oven and immediately drizzle with the Cherry syrup. Set aside to cool. Kept in an airtight container, these will last for 2–3 days.

# Chocolate chip biscuits

**THE GUT FACTOR** CONTAINS *BIFIDOBACTERIUM* AND *LACTOBACILLUS*. SERVED WITH A LIVE PROBIOTIC ICE CREAM
**SUGGESTED BOTANICAL BLEND** NO. 7: SPICED OR NO. 9: EASTERN
**PROBIOTIC** SERVE WITH SOURDOUGH VANILLA ICE CREAM

Rich, bittersweet chocolate and cacao powders are an incredible source of polyphenols (which make up to 6 per cent of cacao's dry weight), including flavanols, anthocyanins, flavones, flavanones and isoflavones (page 29). These special antioxidant compounds combat the effects of biological stress in our cells and perform anti-inflammatory functions. What's more, the polyphenols in cacao are another source of sustenance for probiotics *Bifidobacterium* (page 22) and *Lactobacillus* (page 23), which help maintain our gut pH and support beneficial bacteria. And as they break down polyphenols, they even increase the available levels of these compounds for use directly by our body. We use these biscuits to sandwich our kefir-based Sourdough vanilla ice cream for a decadent, gut-friendly treat (page 80).

In a large bowl, mix together the flour, cacao, salt and sugar. Add the egg and extra yolk, along with the butter and starter, and mix until a ball of dough is formed. Add the chopped chocolate and pecan nuts and mix well.

Form the dough into a 20cm (8-inch) long sausage and wrap it in greaseproof paper. Leave the wrapped dough at room temperature overnight.

The next morning, transfer it to the fridge to enable the dough to firm up.

When you're ready to bake, preheat your oven to 180°C/350°F/Gas Mark 4 and grease a baking tray.

Cut the dough into 14–18 slices and place them on the prepared baking tray. Bake for 12–13 minutes. The biscuits will still be soft; resist the temptation to bake them longer because this will make the biscuits dry and crispy.

Leave the biscuits on the baking tray to cool for a few minutes before you transfer them to a wire rack to cool completely.

▶ **STARTER** SWEET OR SOUR

▶ **INGREDIENTS**

225g Botanical blend nos. 7 or 9, or stoneground wholegrain flour
30g raw cacao powder
pinch of salt
120g coconut sugar
1 large egg, plus 1 yolk
150g sweet butter, plus extra for greasing
50g bubbly, lively starter or discard (page 114; see schedule)
150g bittersweet chocolate, chopped into small pieces or chips
45g pecan nuts, left whole
1 tablespoon vanilla essence
1 teaspoon freshly grated nutmeg

▶ **DDT** 22°C (72°F)

▶ **SCHEDULE**

| | | |
|---|---|---|
| Day 1 | 9pm | Refresh starter (first build) |
| Day 2 | 8am | Refresh starter (second build) |
| | 8pm | Mix dough and return the starter to the fridge (unless you are proceeding to a third build). Wrap the dough and prove overnight |
| Day 3 | 8am | Transfer the dough to the fridge to firm up |
| | | When ready, slice and bake |

Tip I like to change the Botanical blend each time I make these, so feel free to play.

# Sourdough kisses

**THE GUT FACTOR** THESE CONTAIN FLAVONOIDS THAT NOURISH POSITIVE GUT MICROBES, INCREASE FIBRE AND FEED *BIFIDOBACTERIUM*
**SUGGESTED BOTANICAL BLEND** YOUR CHOICE OF BLENDS NO. 2–10
**PROBIOTIC** SERVE WITH KEFIR

I'm not going go to say much at all about these, other than you are getting 20 ingredients in one kiss, and that chocolate has been shown to improve microbes associated with better mood: *Bifidobacterium*. These kisses are a delicious wholegrain treat that delivers fibre and flavonoids in one bite. They are so good; easy to make, crunchy, sweet and sour. It's absolutely impossible to walk past a bowl of these without eating one.

In a large bowl, mix together all the ingredients (except the chocolate and *fleur de sel*) to form a dough. Cover and leave to ferment overnight on the worksurface.

The following morning, test the consistency of the mixture—it should drop off a spoon easily. If needed, add a little water, 10g at a time, to let down to an easily pipeable consistency (see Note).

Preheat the oven to 150°C/300°F/Gas Mark 2 and line 4 baking sheets with baking parchment. Lightly oil the parchment. Put the mixture in a pastry bag and pipe out 4-5cm (1½–2-inch) wide pretzel shapes on to the prepared baking sheets.

Put the trays in the oven (you will need to work in batches) and immediately reduce the temperature to 100°C/210°F/Gas Mark ¼. Bake for 25–30 minutes. The baking time will depend on how thickly you have piped the shapes. When ready, they should be snappable/biscuit-like.

When the kisses are baked, turn the oven off and open the door. Leave the baking sheet in the oven for about 15 minutes so that the kisses continue to dry out in the warm temperature. When the kisses are completely cool and totally dry, remove them very carefully from the baking sheet.

While the kisses are drying out, you can temper the chocolate. Melt 200g of the chocolate in a bowl set over a pan of simmering water on the hob. Bring the temperature up to 50°C (122°F), then turn off the heat and stir in the remaining 100g chocolate. As the temperature drops to 31°C (88°F), dip the kisses in the chocolate to coat. Set aside while the chocolate sets, and as it does so sprinkle the kisses with the *fleur de sel*. The kisses will keep in an airtight container for up to 3 weeks.

## ▶ STARTER SWEET OR SOUR

## ▶ INGREDIENTS
200g bubbly, lively starter or discard (page 114; see schedule)
100g your choice of Botanical blends no.2–10
100g stoneground wholegrain flour
100g water, plus an additional 10–20g if needed
oil, for greasing

## ▶ TO DECORATE
300g bittersweet chocolate, chopped into small chunks (see Tip)
4g *fleur de sel*, to decorate (optional)

*You will need a food thermometer and a pastry bag and tube*

## ▶ DDT 22°C (72°F)

## ▶ SCHEDULE
| | | |
|---|---|---|
| Day 1 | 9pm | Refresh starter (first build) |
| Day 2 | 8am | Refresh starter (second build) |
| | 8pm | Mix dough and return the starter to the fridge (unless you are proceeding to a third build). Prove dough overnight |
| Day 3 | 8am | Pipe and bake |
| Day 3 | 9.30am | Drizzle with chocolate |

Tip **If you are trying to reduce the amount of sugar in your diet, you can use a 100 per cent cocoa solids chocolate, or choose not to use chocolate at all.**

NOTE **The amount of water required depends on the type of flour and the length of time since your starter was refreshed. Use my essential baking advice (pages 119–120) as guidance.**

# Sourdough jalebi

**THE GUT FACTOR** IMPROVED COGNITIVE FUNCTION, INCREASED GUT MICROBIAL DIVERSITY AND ANTI-INFLAMMATORY PROPERTIES.
**SUGGESTED BOTANICAL BLEND** NO. 8: ORIENTAL OR NO. 9: EASTERN
**PROBIOTIC** CHERRY SYRUP

▶ **STARTER** SWEET OR SOUR

▶ **FOR DEEP-FRYING**
750ml (1½ pints) sunflower oil, for deep-frying

▶ **FOR THE DOUGH**
200g Botanical blend nos. 8 or 9 (page 57), or stoneground wholegrain flour
40g banana flour
40g bubbly, lively starter or discard (page 114; see schedule)
½ teaspoon vanilla powder
140g kefir
150g water plus an additional 10–20g if needed at 10°C (50°F), plus approx. 60g extra to let it down
3g sea salt
12–15 saffron strands
1 teaspoon dried turmeric or 2 tablespoons of freshly grated turmeric root
3–4 turns of a black pepper mill

▶ **FOR THE SYRUP**
100ml (3½fl oz) Cherry syrup (page 87)
20g Wild vinegar (page 90)

*You will need a pastry bag and size 7, 8 or 9 piping tube*

▶ **DDT** 21°C (70°F)

▶ **SCHEDULE**

| | | |
|---|---|---|
| Day 1 | 9pm | Refresh starter (first build) |
| Day 2 | 8am | Refresh starter (second build) |
| | 8pm | Mix dough and return the starter to the fridge (unless you are proceeding to a third build) |
| | | Prove the batter overnight |
| Day 3 | 8am | Transfer the batter to the fridge for 1 hour |
| | 9am | Let down the batter to pipeable consistency and fry |

One of my favourite things to eat are *jalebis*, incredibly sweet Indian and Bangladeshi treats. My alternative version uses a diversity wholegrain flour and polyphenol-rich probiotic syrup. They are complex, sweet, a little tart and a joy to eat. Turmeric is a rich source of curcumin, a polyphenol with antioxidant and anti-inflammatory properties that benefit the heart, brain and lungs. The active compound curcumin can also increase the diversity of species in the gut microbiome. Turmeric has also been shown to help arthritis, and studies have also shown that it can improve mood, alertness and memory. To unlock the power of fat-soluble curcumin, we have paired it with pepper, as this increases its bioavailability by 2,000 per cent especially when consumed with fats or oils. Banana flour is high in resistant starch, further benefiting your gut with more prebiotics.

In a large bowl, mix all the dough ingredients except the extra 60g water. If you are using fresh turmeric, add an extra tablespoon of banana flour. Cover the bowl and leave overnight on the worksurface.

The next morning, transfer the fermented dough to the fridge for 1 hour to make it easier to pipe. When you're ready, mix together the Cherry syrup and vinegar and warm gently in a saucepan over a low heat. Heat the oil to 180°C (356°F) in a large, deep saucepan over a medium heat, ready for frying.

Let down the dough by adding 10g of the extra 60g water at a time until it is an easily pipeable consistency; you may not need it all. The amount of water needed depends on how broken down your dough is. Fill a pastry bag with the jalebi batter. Squeeze the contents of the pastry bag into the hot oil in concentric circles, moving from inside to outside.

Fry until the jalebis are crisp and golden, then remove from the oil with a slotted spoon. Next, while they are still warm, drop the jalebis into the syrup mixture for 1 minute, then remove from the syrup and place to dry out on a wire rack.

In all honesty, I have no idea how long these will keep because they always get eaten right away! But I'd suggest eating the same day you make them.

# Chocolate, tangerine & pistachio cakes

**THE GUT FACTOR** PROTECT THE GUT AGAINST MICROBIAL AND FUNGAL CONTAMINATION

**SUGGESTED BOTANICAL BLEND** NO. 5: GOLDEN OR NO. 9: EASTERN

▶ **STARTER** SWEET OR SOUR

▶ **FOR THE DOUGH**

100g Botanical blend no. 5 or no. 9

150g bubbly, lively starter or discard (page 114; see schedule) refreshed with Botanical blend no. 5

30g coconut sugar

30g sunflower oil

1 egg

a little coconut oil and flour, for greasing and dusting

2 tablespoons runny raw honey, for drizzling

▶ **FOR THE JELLO**

zest and juice of 2 Seville oranges (see Tips) and 3 tangerines (this should give you 200g juice)

100g homemade marmalade (or use 100g orange juice. Note that you'll need to increase the quantity of gelatin/agar agar proportionately

3 standard-sized gelatin leaves (or agar agar)

30g coconut sugar

coconut oil, for greasing

▶ **TO FINISH**

200g bittersweet chocolate, chopped into small chunks

3 tablespoons chopped pistachios

*You will need a food thermometer*

**DDT** 23°C (73°F)

▶ **SCHEDULE**

Day 1  9pm  Refresh starter (first build)

Day 2  8am  Refresh starter (second build)

  8pm  Mix dough and return the starter to the fridge (unless you are proceeding to a third build). Prove overnight

Day 3  8am  Make jello

  8.30am  Transfer dough to tins and leave to prove

  10am  Cut out jello discs

  10.30am Bake the cakes

  11am  Once cooled, assemble the cakes

Like all citrus, the delicious, sweet flesh of tangerines is a source of vitamin C, but in this recipe, I am more interested in their skin, because it contains essential oils with myriad properties. Not only do these have the potential to protect against microbial and fungal contamination, but they also have antioxidant functions. Citrus oils are particularly known for their antibacterial activity and their ability to carry aromas associated with reduced symptoms of anxiety and a sense of wellbeing.

These cakes are so good. The chocolate snaps as you bite it, and the light, grainy texture of the cake is is balanced by a soft orange jello. This jello is oh-so-tart, especially when made with Seville oranges and tangerines. The fermentation reduces the sugar in the dough, and the bittersweet chocolate is full of flavonoids. Truthfully though, I don't really care if these are good for me. I just want to eat them!

In a large bowl, mix together the starter, Botanical blend, coconut sugar, sunflower oil and egg, beating the mixture really well. Leave the bowl, covered, on the worksurface overnight.

The next morning, make the jello. Line a 30 x 24cm (12 x 9½-inch) baking tray with greaseproof paper and lightly grease it with a fine layer of coconut oil.

Put the orange and tangerine zest and juice and the marmalade in a small saucepan and warm over a gentle heat. Prepare the gelatin leaves or agar agar by soaking according to the packet instructions.

Stir the coconut sugar into the warmed orange mixture, let cool for 2 minutes, then add the prepared gelatin or agar agar. Pour the jello mixture into the tray and leave in the fridge for about 2 hours to set.

While the jello is setting, grease and flour two 12-hole muffin tins; be generous with the greasing, otherwise the bases may stick. Very gently transfer about 1 tablespoon of dough into each of the prepared holes in the tins. Leave to prove for 2 hours.

**If you can't get Seville oranges then use ordinary ones.**

These cakes are best when they are freshly baked, but as an alternative you can store the cooled bases in an airtight container overnight, then temper the chocolate and assemble the cakes the following morning.

I like to use 100g marmalade rather than extra juice in the jello because it has chunks of candied orange zest in it, and orange peel contains minerals including calcium, copper, magnesium, vitamin A, folate and other B vitamins, as well as dietary fibre.

Once the jello has set, dip a cookie cutter in boiling water, then cut small discs from the jello sheet. The discs need to be a little bit smaller than the dough bases. Use a palette knife to carefully lift the discs away from the paper and place on another tray lined with greaseproof paper. Set aside until needed.

Preheat the oven to 180°C/350°F/Gas Mark 4. Everybody's oven is different, so it's worth checking and making sure you have your oven at the right temperature with this bake. The bases are very small and can easily burn. Bake the bases for about 8 minutes. Leave them to cool in the tins for 2–3 minutes, then carefully remove and place them on to a wire rack. Return the wire rack to the oven (make sure it is turned off). Leave the bases in there for 5–6 minutes, then open the door wide and leave the bases inside for another 5–6 minutes. This final drying stage will give your bases a dry texture that will contrast so beautifully with the soft jello and crisp chocolate. Remove from the oven and leave the bases to cool completely. Once cool, drizzle lightly with the honey.

Meanwhile, temper the chocolate. Melt 150g of the chocolate in a bowl set over a pan of simmering water on the hob. Bring the temperature up to 65°C (149°F), then turn off the heat and stir in the remaining 50g chocolate.

As the bases cool, so too does the temperature of your chocolate. When it drops to 31°C (88°F), it's time to assemble the cakes. Pop a jello disc onto the centre of each base, leaving about 2–3mm uncovered around the edge. Pour tempered chocolate over the tops and finish with chopped pistachios. Leave to set for 10 minutes.

These will keep for up to 1 week in an airtight container.

# Dukkha

**Note: If you suffer from IBS, you should avoid seeds.**

Place the seeds, pistachios and almonds in a dry frying pan over a low heat and lightly toast until fragrant and golden. Allow to cool, then add the remaining ingredients.

Transfer to a jar or airtight container. This dukkha will keep for 1 week in the fridge if you add mint, and for longer if you don't. Use in recipes including Honey, orange & dukkha sweet pappardelle (page 132) and Morello cherry shortbread (page 137).

MAKES 150G **DIVERSITY SCORE** 5
(6 IF YOU ADD MINT)

▶ **INGREDIENTS**
25g (1oz) sesame seeds
50g (1¾oz) pistachios, finely chopped
50g (1¾oz) almonds, finely chopped
20g (¾oz) coconut or white sugar
¼ teaspoon vanilla powder
4–5 (3¼-inch) sprigs of mint, finely chopped (optional)

# Blackberry & cultured cream mini cakes

**THE GUT FACTOR** VERY HIGH LEVELS OF POLYPHENOLS, INCLUDING ANTHOCYANIN, MADE MORE BIOAVAILABLE BY THE FERMENTATION PROCESS.
**SUGGESTED BOTANICAL BLEND** NO. 4: BLUE
**PROBIOTIC** CULTURED CREAM

▶ **STARTER** SWEET OR SOUR

▶ **INGREDIENTS**

250g Botanical blend no. 4 (page 56) or
    stoneground wholegrain flour
200g ground almonds
200g bubbly, lively starter or discard (page 114;
    see schedule)
125g sweet butter, softened, plus extra
    for greasing
125g sunflower oil
125g superfine sugar
zest of 2 lemons
6 medium eggs, at room temperature
1 tablespoon vanilla essence
4 tablespoons barley malt syrup, let down with
    about 10g hot water, to drizzle

▶ **TO FINISH**

240g Blackberry fresh fruit compote (page 83)
1 tablespoon Wild vinegar (page 90)
    or any live vinegar
Cultured cream (page 72)

▶ **DDT** 23°C (73°F)

▶ **SCHEDULE**

Day 1  9pm    Refresh starter (first build)
Day 2  8am    Refresh starter (second build)
       8pm    Mix dough and return the starter to
              the fridge (unless you are proceeding
              to a third build). Prepare your Cultured
              cream. Prove/ferment overnight
Day 3  8am    Bake

Based on miniature Victoria sandwich cakes, these exquisite cakes are full of blackberry compote and lightly sour cultured cream. The blackberries contain high levels of polyphenols including anthocyanin, which is known to positively impact *Akkermansia muciniphila*. This is one of the key gut microbes that helps to maintain the integrity of the gut lining. I have used Botanical blend no. 4, which provides even more polyphenols. The bioavailability of polyphenols, especially anthocyanins, is generally low, but fermentation is well reported to increase the bioavailability of these key nutrients, making them more nourishing. You can further increase the bioavailability of these polyphenols by adding a tablespoon of vinegar to your compote.

Place the flour, ground almonds, starter, butter, sunflower oil, sugar, lemon zest and eggs into a large mixing bowl. Mix them well, making sure all the ingredients are combined, but avoid beating them.

Grease 2 x 12-hole muffin tins with butter and dust them with a very light coating of flour. Divide the cake mixture equally between the tins. Cover and prove overnight on the worksurface.

Once the cakes have doubled in size, preheat your oven to 180°C/350°F/Gas Mark 4. Bake for 18–20 minutes until the cakes are golden around the edges, and a skewer inserted into the centre comes out clean.

Leave to cool in the tins for a few minutes, then gently remove them and put them on a wire rack. Drizzle with the let-down barley malt syrup. Cover the cakes with a clean dish towel, so they don't dry out as they cool.

Once completely cooled, slice them in half to form the two layers of a small sandwich cake. I tend to put the prettier side up. Mix the vinegar into the compote and dollop a spoonful onto the bottom layer of each cake. On what will be the inner side of the top layer, spread some Cultured cream. Sandwich the two layers together. Best enjoyed fresh.

# Poppy seed & lemon cake

**THE GUT FACTOR** POPPY SEEDS ARE A SOURCE OF TOCOPHEROLS AND LINOLEIC ACID.
**SUGGESTED BOTANICAL BLEND** NO. 5: GOLDEN
**PREBIOTIC** RAW HONEY

These ancient seeds have been used by many civilisations, including the Egyptians, Minoans and Sumerians. Still popular in Eastern bakeries, the poppy seed is a beautiful addition to many bakes. They are a rich source of tocopherols, which the body can turn into vitamins E, B1, B3 and B5, as well as calcium and potassium. They are also a source of linoleic acid, an essential polyunsaturated fatty acid. Research indicates that poppy seeds may even help prevent some types of cancer. A high intake of poppy seeds can put you at risk of testing positive on a drug test for opiates, so consume with moderation! Remember that sufferers of IBS should avoid seeds.

Put all the dough ingredients in a large bowl, including the 100g water in which you soaked the saffron. Mix well to combine.

Grease and line a 24cm (9½-inch) square cake tin with greased baking parchment. Transfer the dough to the prepared tin, then cover and leave on the kitchen worksurface overnight, or until doubled in size.

In the morning, preheat your oven to 170°C/340°F/Gas Mark 3½. Mix together the lemon juice, butter and honey to make a syrup. Bake the cake for 25 minutes, then reduce the temperature to 150°C/300°F/Gas Mark 2, cover the top of the cake with foil and bake for a further 15–20 minutes until golden brown and a skewer inserted into the centre comes out clean.

Remove from the oven and use a skewer to poke holes in the top of the cake. Drizzle immediately with the syrup whilst still in the tin.

After 5 minutes, remove from the tin and transfer the cake to a wire rack to cool completely. The honey syrup keeps the cake from going stale, so it will keep in an airtight container for 2–3 days.

▶ **STARTER** SWEET OR SOUR

▶ **FOR THE DOUGH**
400g Botanical blend no. 5 (page 56) or stoneground wholegrain flour, sifted
200g bubbly, lively starter or discard (page 114; see schedule)
125g coconut sugar
100g sunflower oil
2 eggs, beaten, plus 4 extra yolks, at room temperature
zest of 2 large lemons
9g salt
12 saffron strands, soaked in 100g water for 6–8 hours before use
30g poppy seeds (do not add if you suffer from IBS)

▶ **FOR THE TIN**
12g butter
1 heaped tablespoon flour (any Botanical blend or wholemeal)

▶ **FOR THE SYRUP**
juice of 2 lemons
30g butter, softened
2 large tablespoons raw, unpasteurized runny honey

▶ **DDT** 22–23°C (72–73°F)

▶ **SCHEDULE**
Day 1  9pm   Refresh starter (first build)
Day 2  8am   Refresh starter (second build)
       8pm   Mix dough and return the starter to the fridge (unless you are proceeding to a third build)
             Prove overnight
Day 3  8am   Bake

▶ **STARTER** SWEET OR SOUR

▶ **FOR THE DOUGH**

200g bubbly, lively starter or discard (page 114;
    see schedule)

100g finely grated carrots

125g kefir

70g jaggery or coconut sugar

175g sweet butter, melted and cooled to
    26°C (78°F), plus extra for greasing

2 tablespoons orange blossom water

4 free-range eggs, at room temperature

1 teaspoon Ndali vanilla powder

400g Botanical blend no.5 (page 56) or stone-
    ground wholegrain flour, plus extra for dusting

100g wholegrain Khorasan flour

10g fine sea salt

20–40g water, to let down

250g dried mango, soaked in water for
    2–3 hours and drained

60g pumpkin seeds (optional; do not add
    if you suffer from IBS), soaked
    in water overnight and drained

▶ **TO FINISH**

150g Honey, ginger & orange syrup (page 87)

1 tablespoon orange blossom water

▶ **TO SERVE**

Apricot Fresh fruit compote (page 83)

Cultured cream (page 72)

*You will need one 25 x 6cm (12-cup) bundt tin. You
can also use a 24cm (9cm deep) cake tin with a loose
base, but you may need to adjust the baking time.*

▶ **DDT** 23°C (73°F)

▶ **SCHEDULE**

Day 1  9pm    Refresh starter (first build)
Day 2  8am    Refresh starter (second build)
       8pm    Mix dough and return the starter to
              the fridge (unless you are proceeding
              to a third build). Prepare your Cultured
              cream. Prove/ferment overnight
Day 3  8am    Bake

# Golden orange blossom cake

**THE GUT FACTOR** CONTAINS BETA-CAROTENE
**SUGGESTED BOTANICAL BLEND** NO. 5: GOLDEN
**PROBIOTIC** SERVE WITH CULTURED CREAM

Evidence is emerging that the health of the gut microbiota can influence neurodegenerative diseases through various metabolic pathways. I am often asked if there is any way to influence the gut microbes that can influence the brain. It is difficult to identify a single food that has any major impact, as there are few human trials. What is clear is the importance of antioxidants, one of which is beta-carotene, a carotenoid. Carotenoids may benefit the brain by supporting the gut, calming an inflammatory response by the immune system. Studies suggest this may help prevent or delay the development of gut dysbiosis (page 16). This simple and delicious cake, with Botanical blend no. 5, carrots and mangos, has high levels of carotenoids.

Place all the dough ingredients except the water, mango slices and pumpkin seeds in a large mixing bowl and stir until they are all incorporated. It is not necessary to beat the mixture; it just needs to be smooth. Add the water a little at a time to let down the mixture slightly. The amount you need will vary depending on the fibre levels in your flour.

Grease your tin with butter and dust it with flour. Arrange the mango slices and pumpkin seeds in the base of the tin, and then pour in the batter. Cover and leave on the worksurface in the kitchen overnight

The next day, preheat the oven to 170°C/340°F/Gas Mark 3½. Bake the cake for 30–35 minutes, until it turns a lovely golden color. Check for doneness using a skewer—it should come out clean when you insert it into the thickest part of the cake. If the cake is not fully baked, return it to the oven for another few minutes, then test again. You may need to turn the oven down or place foil over the cake, if you need to cook it for longer, to avoid burning the top.

Once it is baked, let the cake cool in the tin briefly, then turn out onto a plate. Use a skewer to lightly poke some holes in the top of the cake, then gently drizzle the syrup over the cake a spoonful at a time, allowing it to soak up the liquid. Cover with a large mixing bowl, which will retain some of the steam while the cake cools completely. This cake is delicious served freshly baked, with Apricot compote and Cultured cream.

## ▶ STARTER SWEET OR SOUR

### ▶ INGREDIENTS

200g bubbly, lively starter or discard (page 114;
   see schedule)

150g sunflower oil

5 tablespoons date syrup

zest of 3 oranges and juice of 1 orange

100ml Earl Grey tea

100g soft light brown sugar

3 eggs, at room temperature

200g carrots, grated

100g walnuts, finely chopped

500g Botanical blend nos. 7 or 9, or
   stoneground wholegrain flour, sifted

2 teaspoons Ndali vanilla powder

1 teaspoon freshly grated nutmeg

butter, for greasing

3 tablespoons Diversity muesli (page 58),
   with fruit removed

### ▶ FOR THE PROBIOTIC CREAM FROSTING

150g Cultured butter, at room temperature

40g malt (optional)

1kg Malted orange labneh (page 76), at
   room temperature

3 teaspoons Ndali vanilla extract

zest of 2 oranges

### ▶ TO DECORATE

50g walnuts, chopped

3–4 tablespoons date syrup

### ▶ DDT 22–23°C (72–73°F)

### ▶ SCHEDULE

| | | |
|---|---|---|
| Day 1 | 9pm | Refresh starter (first build) |
| Day 2 | 8am | Refresh starter (second build) |
| | 8pm | Mix dough and return the starter to the fridge (unless you are proceeding to a third build). Prove overnight |
| Day 3 | 9am | Bake |
| | 11am | Decorate |

# Carrot & walnut cake

**THE GUT FACTOR** INCREASES LEVELS OF POLYPHENOLS
**SUGGESTED BOTANICAL BLEND** NO. 7: SPICED OR
NO. 9: EASTERN
**PROBIOTIC** PROBIOTIC CREAM FROSTING

Most problems in life seem smaller when faced with a pot of tea, a slice of cake and time to chat. Here, I've combined Earl Grey with walnuts and a malt frosting for a gut microbiome-friendly version of a carrot cake. Black tea is a powerhouse of polyphenols like catechins, theaflavins and arubigens. These antioxidant compounds help prevent oxidative stress in the cells, which can also help mood and attention span. Studies show that the polyphenols in tea can help reduce the risk of stroke and cardiovascular diseases, as well as having antidepressant properties. Walnuts are also a source of polyphenols and ellagic acid, which is metabolized by gut microbes into anti-inflammatory compounds. One study suggested that the undigestible fibre in walnuts provides food for bacterial species in the gut that promote health and reduce inflammation.

In a large mixing bowl, mix together the starter, oil, syrup, orange zest, tea and sugar until smooth. In a separate bowl or small jug, beat the eggs until frothy, then stir them into the mixture. Add the orange juice, grated carrot and walnuts. Add the flour, vanilla powder and nutmeg and stir, ensuring everything is fully incorporated.

Grease 3 x 20cm (8-inch) round cake tins with butter and dust with muesli. Divide the mixture evenly between the tins, cover and leave overnight on the worksurface. In the morning, the cakes will be risen to double their previous size. Preheat the oven to 180°C/350°F/Gas Mark 4.

Bake the cakes for 20–25 minutes, or until they are light golden and a skewer inserted into the sponge comes out clean. Turn off the oven, open the oven door and leave the cakes in the oven for 5 minutes to dry. Remove from the oven and leave to cool in the tins.

While the cakes are cooling, make the frosting. Place the butter, malt, labneh, vanilla extract and orange zest into a bowl and stir with a wooden spoon until it forms a paste. Now whisk using a hand or electric whisk until smooth and thoroughly blended.

Once completely cool, spread a third of the icing on one cake, place a second cake on top and spread with another third of the frosting. Place the remaining cake on top and spread with the remaining third of the frosting. Decorate with chopped walnuts and drizzle with date syrup. Eat fresh.

# Chocolate brownie cake

**THE GUT FACTOR** INCREASE IN THE GROWTH OF BOTH *LACTOBACILLUS SPP.* AND *BIFIDOBACTERIUM.*
**SUGGESTED BOTANICAL BLEND** NO. 7: SPICED
**PROBIOTIC** SERVE WITH CULTURED CREAM

▶ **STARTER** SWEET OR SOUR

▶ **INGREDIENTS**

100g soft, moist pitted dates
150g bubbly, lively starter or discard (page 114; see schedule)
100g olive oil
100g sunflower oil
150g muscovado sugar
100g 85 per cent cocoa solids bittersweet chocolate, melted
50g butter, softened, plus extra for greasing
4 large eggs, at room temperature
60g raw organic unsweetened chocolate powder
185g Botanical blend no. 7, sifted malt flour or einkorn flour, plus extra for dusting
3g sea salt
1 teaspoon vanilla powder
1 teaspoon freshly grated nutmeg

▶ **TO DECORATE**

50g each of bittersweet chocolate, white chocolate and milk chocolate, to drizzle (optional)
1 tablespoon unsweetened chocolate powder
1 tablespoon malt powder

▶ **DDT** 23°C (73°F)

▶ **SCHEDULE**

Day 1  9pm    Refresh starter (first build)
Day 2  8am    Refresh starter (second build)
         8pm    Mix dough and return the starter to the fridge (unless you are proceeding to a third build).
                      Prepare your Cultured cream.
                      Prove/ferment overnight
Day 3  8am    Bake

This rich, fudgy cake is easy to make, and it's official: chocolate is good for mental health. Scientists at University College London discovered that people who reported enjoying bittersweet chocolate were significantly less likely to report any clinical signs of depression. The research team also said that their study doesn't prove that bittersweet chocolate can cure depression. But chocolate contains several psychoactive ingredients, including two forms of anandamine, which results in a feeling of euphoria comparable to that of cannabis. Bittersweet chocolate also has more antioxidants than milk chocolate, which reduce inflammation in the body, a reaction that some experts believe is linked to depression. In early studies, cocoa has been shown to modify the gut microbiome and bring health benefits. One study showed consumption of cocoa induced a significant increase in the growth of both *Lactobacillus* spp. and *Bifidobacterium*. Cocoa also has high levels of flavonoids (page 29). It is important to use raw, organic cocoa.

Mash the dates in a large mixing bowl. It doesn't matter if they are not fully broken down, but if you prefer you can use a blender to chop them finely. Add the leaven, oils and muscovado sugar and mix. Make sure that the melted chocolate has cooled slightly, then add it along with the butter; the warm chocolate will help the butter to melt. Add the eggs and mix again. Now sieve together the cocoa powder, flour, salt, vanilla powder and nutmeg and add to the mixture. Mix well.

Grease and line a 20cm (8-inch) round baking tin with greased baking parchment. Transfer the mixture to the tin. Cover it with foil and leave on the kitchen worksurface to prove overnight. The following morning, preheat the oven to 160°C/325°F/Gas Mark 3. Bake the cake for 30–35 minutes, without removing its covering of foil. This cake should be firm on top, but very yielding as it is gorgeously squidgy. Leave to cool and set in the tin.

When you are ready to serve, melt the bittersweet, milk and white chocolate in separate bowls set over barely simmering water. In another bowl, mix together the unsweetened chocolate powder and malt powder. Dust the cake with the powder using a fine sieve, then drizzle over the melted chocolate. Serve with Cultured cream (page 72).

# Yemarina yewotet dabo (Ethiopian honey & buttermilk bread)

**THE GUT FACTOR** HONEY MAY ENHANCE PROBIOTIC EFFICACY AGAINST PATHOGENS IN THE GUT. BANANAS CAN REDUCE BLOATING AND INCREASE *BIFIDOBACTERIUM*
**SUGGESTED BOTANICAL BLEND** NO. 7: SPICED
**PROBIOTIC** UNPASTEURIZED HONEY

This voluptuous bread is made with barley, buttermilk and rosemary. Rosemary is a stunningly fragrant herb and a potent therapeutic that can relax the muscles of the gut and the windpipe (trachea), while also protecting the liver. It also has antioxidant properties thanks to the polyphenol caffeic acid and its rosemary-specific derivative, rosmarinic acid. Research indicates the rosmarinic acid may have therapeutic applications, including inflammatory disease, liver toxicity, heart disease, peptic ulcers and asthma. Honey has significant potential gut benefits (see page 84). Bananas, meanwhile contain resistant starch (page 27) and fructo-oligosaccharides (page 26). One trial studying gastrointestinal symptoms in women eating bananas revealed significantly lower bloating levels in the banana group (compared with the non-banana group), and a slight increase in *Bifidobacterium*.

▶ **STARTER** SWEET OR SOUR

▶ **INGREDIENTS**

2 eggs, at room temperature, beaten
6g salt
125g runny honey
200g bubbly, lively starter or discard (page 114; see schedule)
250g buttermilk
100g sweet butter, melted and cooled to room temperature, plus extra for greasing
40g water, plus an additional 10–20g if needed
500g Botanical blend no. 7 or stoneground wholegrain flour, sifted
semolina flour, for dusting
3 tablespoons mixed seeds (optional; do not add if you suffer from IBS)
1 banana, finely sliced
1 teaspoon coconut sugar (optional)

▶ **TO FINISH**

50g unpasteurized honey
Needles from a 6-inch sprig of rosemary, finely chopped with 1g (a pinch) of sea salt and then ground to a paste using a pestle and mortar
1 tablespoon sweet butter

▶ **DDT** 22°C (72°F)

▶ **SCHEDULE**

| | | |
|---|---|---|
| Day 1 | 9pm | Refresh starter (first build) |
| Day 2 | 8am | Refresh starter (second build) and infuse honey with rosemary |
| | 8pm | Mix dough and return the starter to the fridge (unless you are proceeding to a third build). Prove overnight |
| Day 3 | 8am | Bake |

In a large bowl, beat together the eggs, salt and honey until they form a smooth mixture. Add the starter and stir. Then add the buttermilk, butter, and water and mix well. Finally, add the flour and mix.

Grease and line a 1kg loaf tin with greased baking parchment and dust with semolina. Sprinkle the tin with the seeds, if using. Turn the dough into the tin. Cover and leave on the kitchen worksurface overnight.

The next day, preheat the oven to 180°C/350°F/Gas Mark 4. The dough should be well-risen and delicate. Top with the banana slices and sprinkle with the coconut sugar, if using. Bake for 30 minutes, then place a piece of foil on top to protect it from burning and return to the oven for a further 15 minutes, or until the loaf is a light golden brown and cooked through. Remove from the oven and cool on a wire rack.

Mix the rosemary, honey and butter in a small bowl and drizzle this mixture over the loaf while it is still warm. This is delicious served with Cultured cream (page 72). It will keep for up to 2 days in an airtight container.

▶ **STARTER** SWEET OR SOUR

▶ **FOR THE PASTRY**

400g Botanical blend no.7 (page 57) or
  stoneground wholegrain flour

50g bubbly, lively starter or discard (page 114;
  see schedule)

5g sea salt

50g coconut sugar

220g sweet butter, plus extra for greasing

3 egg yolks, at room temperature

1 egg, beaten with 1 tablespoon of milk or
  watered down kefir, to glaze.

▶ **FOR THE FILLING**

30g sweet butter

900g (total) 4 different varieties of apple, including
  small sweet dessert apples, cored and sliced
  into 2-mm (¹/₁₆-inch) slices, skins left on, plus
  1 extra apple, peeled, cored and grated

25g muscovado sugar

1½ teaspoons (total) mixed ground spices (e.g.
  cinnamon, nutmeg, cloves, black pepper,
  allspice, cardamom)

50g ground almonds

▶ **DDT** 23°C (73°F)

▶ **SCHEDULE**

Day 1  9pm    Refresh starter (first build)
Day 2  8am    Refresh starter (second build)
       8pm    Mix dough and return the starter to
              the fridge (unless you are
              proceeding to a third build). Divide
              the dough. Roll out the smaller piece
              and chill for 30 minutes. Prepare
              your Cultured cream and leave it
              to ferment overnight
       8:45 pm Slice the chilled smaller piece of
              dough into strips. Leave the larger
              ball of dough and the dough strips
              to prove overnight
Day 3  8am    Sauté the apples and assemble
              the pie
       8.30am Bake

# Four-apple pie

**THE GUT FACTOR** APPLES ARE FULL OF PECTIN, WHICH
NOURISHES *LACTOBACILLUS* AND *BIFIDOBACTERIUM*.
**SUGGESTED BOTANICAL BLEND** NO. 7: SPICED
**PROBIOTIC** SERVE WITH CULTURED CREAM

In autumn I often put my students to work harvesting apples. There
are about a dozen varieties in our orchard, each with a different fibre
structure. This recipe uses four varieties of apple; each one counts toward
the diversity score. Apples are a source of phytonutrients, including
polyphenols, which are mostly concentrated in their skins. They are also
an excellent source of pectin, a fermentable dietary fibre with gelling
properties that encourage bowel movements, and also nourishes good
bacteria, such as *Lactobacillus* (page 23) and *Bifidobacterium* (page
22). Commercially produced apples are sprayed with large amounts of
pesticides, so it's better to purchase from reliable locals.

To make the pastry, put the flour, starter, salt, sugar and butter in a
mixing bowl and mix until the mixture resembles breadcrumbs. Stir in
the egg yolks and 3–4 tablespoons of very cold water and mix to form a
dough. You may need to add another tablespoon of water.

Divide the dough into two, one piece larger than the other: about 3/5 and
2/5. Roll out the smaller piece to a thickness of about 6mm (¼ inch) and
chill in the fridge for 30 minutes. Cut into 2cm (¾-inch) strips and lay the
strips on a piece of greaseproof paper. Lay another piece of greaseproof
paper on top and cover with a slightly damp dish towel. Leave on the
worksurface overnight. Leave the larger piece of dough in a bowl,
covered, on the worksurface overnight to ferment too.

In the morning, lightly grease a 24cm (9½-inch), 6cm (2½-inch) deep pie
dish. Use your fingers to push the larger piece of pastry into the tin to
form an even base. Put the base in the fridge but leave the pastry strips
on the worksurface. Melt the butter in a large pan over a low heat and
gently sauté the apple slices. Add the grated apple along with the sugar
and spices and cook for 5 minutes until the grated apple is mushy but
the slices are not quite cooked. Taste and add more sugar if required.
Preheat the oven to 180°C/350°F/Gas Mark 4.

Strain any excess liquid off the apples and set them to aside to cool.
Take the base out of the fridge and put a layer of apples in the base,
then sprinkle with ground almonds. Once the pie dish is full, arrange the
pastry strips over the top in a lattice pattern. Brush with the egg wash
and bake for 30 minutes or until golden. Leave to cool, then serve with
Cultured cream (page 72).

# Wild blackberry tarts

**THE GUT FACTOR** INCREASE IN POLYPHENOLS AND
MAINTAIN HEALTHY LEVELS OF *BIFIDOBACTERIUM*.
**SUGGESTED BOTANICAL BLEND** NO. 4: BLUE
**PROBIOTIC** CRÈME PÂTISSIÈRE

It is magical to eat blackberries as you pick them. At the School, part of what we teach about nourishing the gut is actually about taking the time to connect to the ingredients you bake with. There is also strong evidence that getting outside lowers cortisol levels, which when raised can lower levels of the beneficial bacteria *Bifidobacterium*. The flesh and seeds of blackberries are rich sources of polyphenols and fibre, and research has shown they are effective in preventing the oxidative stress and inflammation that play so many roles in human health. Blackberries also feed beneficial bacteria in the gut. Early investigations also indicate that blackberries may be able to support cognitive and motor function in old age and positively influence the gut microbiome in people with obesity, reducing neuroinflammation that plays a role in ageing and neurodegenerative conditions.

▶ **STARTER** SWEET OR SOUR

▶ **FOR THE PASTRY**

50g bubbly, lively starter or discard (page 114;
  see schedule)
200g Botanical blend no. 4 or stoneground
  wholegrain flour
140g sweet butter, diced, plus extra for greasing
3g sea salt
150g ground almonds
50g coconut sugar
1 egg, beaten with 1 tablespoon ice-cold water

▶ **FOR THE FILLING**

400g Blackberry fresh fruit compote (page 83)
375ml (12½ fl oz) Crème pâtissière (page 75)
400g fresh blackberries (or blueberries,
  loganberries, blackcurrants, redcurrants,
  or strawberries)

▶ **DDT** 22°C (72°F)

▶ **SCHEDULE**

| Day 1 | 9pm | Refresh starter (first build) |
| Day 2 | 8am | Refresh starter (second build) |
|  | 8pm | Mix dough and return the starter to the fridge (unless you are proceeding to a third build). Prepare your crème pâtissière. Prove/ferment overnight |
| Day 3 | 8am | Bake |

Tip **If you don't want to serve these right away, the pastry cases will keep for 2–3 days in an airtight container. Just put them in the oven for a few minutes to crisp up again before assembling and serving.**

Put the starter, flour, butter and salt into bowl and use your fingers to mix until it resembles breadcrumbs. Stir in the ground almonds and coconut sugar, then add the egg-and-water mixture and mix until the flour starts to clump together. Bring together with your hands to form a ball.

Knead very gently on a lightly floured worktop until smooth, then shape into a flat disc. Wrap in plastic wrap and leave to ferment overnight on the kitchen worksurface.

The next day, grease and line 2 x 25cm (10-inch), 9cm (3½-inch) deep baking tins with greased baking parchment. Use your fingers to push the pastry into the tins, forming even cases about 3mm thick. Prick the pastry all over with a fork, line each case with baking parchment and fill with baking beans. Leave to rest in the fridge for about 30 minutes.

Preheat the oven to 180°C/350°F/Gas Mark 4. Bake the pastry cases for 12 minutes until the sides have set. Remove the baking beans and baking parchment and bake for another 2 minutes. Transfer to a wire rack. After a few moments, remove from the tins. Turn the oven off and put the pastry cases, on the wire rack, into the oven to dry out for a few minutes.

When you are ready to serve, divide the blackberry compote between the two pastry cases and spread it evenly. Top with the crème pâtissière and scatter liberally with berries. Serve within the hour.

# Raspberry slices

**THE GUT FACTOR** HIGH IN POLYPHENOLS AND FIBRE; HELPS
MAINTAIN HEALTHY LEVELS OF *AKKERMANSIA MUCINIPHILA*
**SUGGESTED BOTANICAL BLEND** NO. 3: RED
**PROBIOTIC** SERVE WITH YOGURT

Your microbes love delectable raspberries. Their bright scarlet pigment
is a tell-tale sign of high polyphenolic content, but they also contain a
good amount of vitamin C and higher levels of fibre than most berries.
Early studies also indicate that raspberries may help increase gut
microbial diversity. Raspberries are believed to be useful in maintaining
healthy levels of *Akkermansia muciniphila*, a bacterium shown to
strengthen the lining of the colon. Manganese is another trace element
found in good levels in the raspberry; it contributes to a number of
metabolic processes including bone health and the synthesis of GABA
(page 19), a compound that helps relieve anxiety and improve mood.
These slices are equally delicious with any other compote in season. You
can also add in about 30g chopped mixed nuts or desiccated coconut.

▶ **STARTER** SWEET OR SOUR

▶ **FOR THE PASTRY**

100g sweet butter, plus extra for greasing
60g coconut sugar
220g Botanical blend no. 3 or stoneground
    wholegrain flour, plus extra for dusting
2g sea salt
40g bubbly, lively starter or discard (page 114;
    see schedule)

▶ **FOR THE FILLING**

235g ground almonds
175g sweet butter
75g coconut sugar
3 eggs, at room temperature
100g leftover sourdough starter from first
    refreshment (page 114)
a few drops bitter almond extract (optional)
350g Raspberry or Cherry fresh fruit compote
    (page 83)
150g fresh raspberries
30g flaked almonds
2g sea salt

▶ **TO SERVE**

Live yogurt (page 72)

▶ **DDT** 22°C (72°F)

▶ **SCHEDULE**

Day 1  9pm  Refresh starter (first build)
Day 2  8am  Refresh starter (second build)
       8pm  Mix dough and return the starter to
            the fridge (unless you are proceeding
            to a third build). Push dough into tin
            and prepare your yogurt.
            Leave to prove/ferment overnight
Day 3  8am  Part blind bake
       8.30am  Fill and bake

Grease a 23 x 23cm (9 x 9 inch) baking tin with butter and dust with flour. In
a large mixing bowl, beat together the butter and sugar until they are light
and creamy. Add the flour, salt and starter and combine to form a dough,
using a drop of water to bring together if necessary.

Tip the dough into the prepared baking tin and use your fingertips to press
it in evenly and pinch a tidy edge around the sides of the tin. Cover and
leave on the kitchen worksurface overnight.

The next morning, preheat the oven to 160°C/325°F/Gas Mark 3. Line the
tin with baking parchment and baking beans. Blind bake the pastry for 10
minutes. Remove from the oven and set on a wire rack to cool.

Increase the oven temperature to 180°C/350°F/Gas Mark 4.

While the base is cooling, make the filling. In a bowl, stir together the
ground almonds, butter, sugar, eggs, leftover starter and bitter almond
extract. Set aside. When the base is cooled, spread it thickly with the
raspberry or cherry compote. Spoon the ground almond mixture onto the
fruit-covered base and gently spread it evenly over the top. Scatter over the
fresh raspberries and flaked almonds.

Bake for 30 minutes, then decrease the oven temperature to 160°C/325°F/
Gas Mark 3 and bake for another 8–10 minutes, until it is a beautiful
golden brown. Leave to cool on a wire rack. Serve with Live yogurt.

▶ **STARTER** SWEET OR SOUR

▶ **FOR THE DOUGH**

50g bubbly, lively starter or discard (page 114;
   see schedule)

50g kefir or yogurt (page 72)

2 medium eggs, at room temperature

35g coconut sugar

75g sweet butter, at room temperature,
   plus extra for greasing

200g Botanical blend no. 8 or 9 or stoneground
   wholegrain flour, sifted

a pinch of salt

30g water, plus an additional 5–10g if needed

zest of 1 lemon

poppy seeds, for dusting (do not add if you suffer
   from IBS)

▶ **TO SERVE**

Cherry syrup (page 87) or other syrup of
   your choice

Sourdough fizz (page 92)

edible flowers, such as hibiscus, chamomile,
   and almond blossom

berries, such as blueberries, raspberries,
   or blackberries

*You will need a tin with moulds that hold about 20g
(¾oz) each, such as a mini muffin tin*

▶ **DDT** 22°C (72°F)

▶ **SCHEDULE**

| | | |
|---|---|---|
| Day 1 | 8pm | Make Sourdough fizz and leave to ferment |
| Day 2 | 8pm | Refresh starter (first build) |
| Day 3 | 8am | Refresh starter (second build) |
| | 8pm | Mix dough and return the starter to the fridge (unless you are proceeding to a third build). Divide dough between moulds and leave to prove overnight |
| Day 4 | 8am | Bake and set aside until needed |
| | 6pm | (Or whenever you wish to serve) Serve with the Sourdough Fizz |

# Cherry bites in fizz

**THE GUT FACTOR** CONTAIN POLYPHENOL-RICH CHERRIES.
**SUGGESTED BOTANICAL BLEND** NO 8: ORIENTAL OR NO 9: EASTERN
**PROBIOTIC** SOURDOUGH FIZZ

These cherry bites are such fun to eat because they are fizzy, so they're a great bake to get children enjoying a gut-friendly treat. Getting an early start to gut health is important; studies have shown that habitual consumption of carbohydrates and fibre affects the balance of bacteria in your gut and potentially influences which species thrive there.

Cherries are rich in polyphenols, and a study has found that a healthier gut microbiota increases the bioavailability of these powerful keys to health when consuming cherries. The results of the study demonstrated that an individual's gut microbiota strongly influences the way the body takes up polyphenol metabolites from the cherries. The conclusion was that the microbiota of individuals consuming a less nourishing diet may have a lower ability to metabolize polyphenols, reducing bioavailability and potential health benefits. The study raised questions about the ability of individuals to uptake powerful metabolites that are key to health depending on their diet when they were younger. So, it makes sense to start baking to nourish as early as possible.

**NOTE:** The Sourdough fizz can take 3 days to ferment, so remember to make it ahead of time.

In a large bowl, cream together the butter and sugar. Add the rest of the dough ingredients and mix to form your dough. Prepare the tin. Generously butter the inside of each mould and dust with poppy seeds. Divide the dough between the prepared moulds, leaving enough room for them to rise.

Leave the filled moulds to prove in a warm area of the kitchen overnight. The dough will rise by a little over half of its original volume.

The next day, preheat the oven to 180°C/350°F/Gas Mark 4. Bake the bites for 15 minutes until golden. Let the bites cool, then carefully remove them from the moulds. Set aside until ready to serve.

To serve, place two bites in a deep bowl. Pour over the cherry syrup. Add any berries or edible flowers, if using. Just before serving, pour the Sourdough fizz over the top of each bowl.

This is the advanced section. The following recipes are intended for confident bakers as they require real technical ability.

**Note:** these recipes are not suitable for people with serious digestive issues as the doughs are not as broken down.

♦ **ADVANCED**   MAKES 2
**DIVERSITY SCORE** INGREDIENTS 7 +
BOTANICAL BLEND 21+ = 28+

▶ **STARTER** SWEET

▶ **FOR THE LEAVEN**
90g Botanical blend no. 1 (page 55)
100g water, plus an additional 10–20g if needed,
    at 34°C (93°F)
60g triple-refreshed sweet starter (page 110)

▶ **FOR THE BRIOCHE**
600g Botanical blend no. 1 (page 55)
150g water, plus an additional 10–20g if needed,
    at 28°C (82°F)
275g egg yolks, at room temperature
25g runny honey
8g salt
250g sweet butter, at room temperature,
    plus extra for greasing
175g coconut sugar or white sugar (please
    note that coconut sugar can be much more
    challenging to work with)
fine polenta, for dusting
1 beaten egg, to glaze

▶ **DDT** 28°C (82°F)

▶ **SCHEDULE**

| Day 1 | 8am | Refresh starter (first build). Make Sourdough fizz and leave to ferment |
| | 9pm | Refresh starter (second build) |
| Day 2 | 8am | Refresh starter (third build) |
| | 6pm | Make leaven |
| | 9pm | Mix dough, then prove overnight and for most of the next day |
| Day 3 | 6pm | Transfer the dough to the fridge |
| | 9pm | Shape the dough and place in tins |
| Day 4 | 8am | Bake |

# Brioche

**THE GUT FACTOR** A MORE MODERATE EFFECT ON BLOOD SUGAR THAN OTHER BRIOCHE RECIPES.
**SUGGESTED BOTANICAL BLEND** NO. 1: HYBRID
**PROBIOTIC** SOURDOUGH FIZZ (PAGE 92)

In brioche, the texture of the dough becomes light and the structure reflects the long-chain sugars that form during fermentation. This long fermentation and inclusion of wholegrain slows down the rate of assimilation of carbohydrates and increases resistant starch. The microbes also convert the sugar into lactic and acetic acid, so this will have a more moderate effect on blood sugar than its white yeasted counterpart.

Make the leaven by mixing together the flour, water and starter. Stir, cover and leave at an ambient temperature for 3 hours. When you are ready to mix the dough, make sure all your ingredients are at room temperature. Place the flour, water, leaven, egg yolks, and honey in the bowl of a stand mixer and use the dough hook on a low speed to combine them. The dough will be stiff. Gradually increase the speed to the highest setting and continue to mix for 8–10 minutes. Add the salt, then reduce the speed to medium and gradually add the butter, mixing well and resting between each addition.

Use the windowpane test (see page 181) to check that the dough is developed. If it needs further development, mix for a few minutes on medium speed and check again. Once fully developed, add the sugar in increments, mixing on a slow speed until incorporated. Cover the bowl and leave on the kitchen worksurface to prove overnight and most of the next day.

Pop the dough in the fridge for about 3 hours before you shape it. Grease two 24 x 12 x 8.5cm (9½ x 4½ x 3¼-inch) good heavy-gauge loaf tins with butter and dust with fine polenta. Remove the dough from the fridge and turn out onto a lightly floured worksurface. Divide into 6 pieces using a dough scraper and roll them up to form into 3 balls for each tin. Place the dough into the tins. Ensure the outer seam is sealed. Cover and leave to prove overnight on the worksurface.

The following day, preheat the oven to 180°C/350°F/Gas Mark 4. Brush the brioche lightly with egg, then bake for 35 minutes. Reduce the oven temperature to 160°C/325°F/Gas Mark 3, and bake for 10 minutes until golden brown. Allow to cool in the tins for a couple of minutes before turning them out onto a wire rack. Serve with Sourdough fizz (page 92). The brioche will keep for 2–3 days wrapped in a dish towel.

▶ **FOR THE WHITE LEAVEN**

60g white roller-milled flour, about 13 per cent protein
68g water at 21°C (70°F)
22g triple-refreshed sweet starter (page 110)

▶ **FOR THE DOUGH**

500g Botanical blend no. 1: Hybrid (page 55), please note that no other blend will work for this recipe
170g water, plus an additional 10–20g if needed, at 28°C (82°F)
125g soft brown sugar
10g fine salt
1 medium egg, plus 1 yolk, at room temperature
30g sweet butter

▶ **FOR THE LAMINATION**

325g sweet butter

▶ **TO FINISH**

1 beaten egg, for the egg wash

▶ **DDT** 27°C (81°F)

▶ **SCHEDULE**

| Day 1 | 8am | Refresh starter (first build) |
| | 9pm | Refresh starter (second build) |
| Day 2 | 8am | Refresh starter (third build) |
| | 10pm | Make leaven |
| Day 3 | 8am | Mix dough and prove at room temperature for 10 hours |
| | 6pm | Transfer to fridge and leave overnight |
| Day 4 | 8am | Laminate the dough and refrigerate |
| | 8pm | Prepare your bake and prove |
| Day 5 | 9am | Bake |

Tip If you roll too thin, over ferment your dough, do not keep it cold enough when you laminate, prove too hot or under prove your final prove, the butter will ooze out when you bake.

# Laminated dough (base recipe)

This recipe is for intermediate–advanced bakers, and creates the base used in the Mille-feuille (page 176), Miso prune Danish (page 175) and the Fig & walnut slices (page 172). Sourdough makes a huge difference to the flavor. Laminating the dough means we are creating layers of fat between layers of dough, which then separate to create a wonderfully light, open, flaky texture when baked. Because we need gluten structure, the technique involves reducing the acidity and building yeast in your starter (see page 114).

To get the strength in the dough for a good lamination, use Botanical blend no. 1, which has a strong, white roller-milled four. You need an osmotolerant starter (see page 108 and the Glossary on page 186) with reduced acidity and the need to retain some gluten structure means that this crisp, defined, laminated dough has a higher gluten load than other bakes in this book.

Use a good-quality butter with a high fat content; the butter I have used has fat content of 83 per cent. Keeping the dough cold between folds is essential. Don't be put off by my list of instructions; I have broken them down into steps to make the method as straightforward as possible. For best results, use the fan setting of a convection oven to bake this dough.

Make the leaven by mixing together the flour, water and starter. Stir, cover and leave at an ambient temperature overnight.

The next day, when you are ready to mix the dough, place all the dough ingredients, along with the leaven into the bowl of a stand mixer except the 325g butter for lamination.

Mix on a low speed until the dough is fully mixed. You need to develop the dough. Form the dough into a ball by hand, cover and prove at room temperature for 8 hours.

By about 6pm the dough will have risen significantly. Lightly oil a 24 x 30cm (9½ –12-inch) tin. Knock back the dough and carefully fold into the prepared tin. Place in the coldest spot in the fridge (5°C/41°F) and refrigerate overnight.

The next day, take your butter for laminating from the fridge. Place between layers of greaseproof paper and use a rolling pin to beat it into

a nice rectangle half the size of the rectangle of dough. Remove the dough from the fridge and take it out of the tin. Place the butter block in the centre of the dough (see photo). Fold in the sides to meet in the middle, enclosing the butter.

Roll the dough into a long rectangle, keeping the finished thickness to 2cm (¾ inch). With the dough lying lengthways away from you, lift one end and fold it two thirds over the dough, then lift the remaining one third and fold this on top of the 2 layers. You now have 3 layers, and this process is known as a single turn (or a letter fold).

Wrap the dough in plastic wrap and place in the fridge for 1 hour. Remove and repeat the single turn. Again, wrap the dough in plastic wrap and return to the fridge for another hour. Repeat the single turn again; you now have a dough with 27 layers.

Return to the fridge. If it is a warm day, pop the dough in the freezer for 20 minutes before the final rolling and shaping. The dough is now ready to use in your chosen recipe.

# Fig & walnut slices

**THE GUT FACTOR** THE MICROBES ARE CENTRAL TO PRODUCTION OF NEUROTRANSMITTERS ASSOCIATED WITH MENTAL HEALTH
**SUGGESTED BOTANICAL BLEND** NO. 1: HYBRID
**PROBIOTIC** CRÈME PÂTISSIÈRE

▶ **STARTER** SWEET

▶ **FOR THE DOUGH**
1 x batch Laminated dough (page 170)
1 egg, beaten, for egg wash
80g Dukkha (page 146)

▶ **FOR THE FILLING**
8 tablespoons Crème pâtissière (page 75)
8 large figs, sliced
20 walnut halves, toasted
raw, unpasteurized honey, to drizzle

▶ **DDT** 27°C (80°F)

▶ **SCHEDULE**

| Day 1 | 8am | Refresh starter (first build) |
|---|---|---|
| | 9pm | Refresh starter (second build) |
| Day 2 | 8am | Refresh starter (third build) |
| | 10pm | Make leaven |
| Day 3 | 8am | Mix dough and prove at room temperature for 10 hours |
| | 6pm | Transfer to fridge and leave overnight |
| Day 4 | 8am | Laminate the dough and refrigerate. Prepare the Crème pâtissière and leave to ferment |
| | 8pm | Cut the dough into slices and prove in the oven overnight |
| Day 5 | 9am | Bake Once cool, add toppings |

Transforming knowledge and studies into something delicious and nourishing that we can eat and enjoy is at the heart of my approach. This classic combination of figs and walnuts, with a live probiotic crème pâtissier, was influenced by the work of two key scientists. Both are leading the way in our understanding of food, microbes, and mood. Professor Felice Jacka has led studies at Deakin University, and her work has shown that people consuming food and drinks high in sugar and sodium are more likely to develop mental health conditions. She has demonstrated that by choosing a healthy diet, it may be possible to boost your mood. John Cryan is a neuroscientist at the University College of Cork in Ireland, and his work on Psychobiotics is changing our understanding of the role of live bacteria on mood. His research indicates that microbes have developed ways to influence their host's behavior for their own ends. Modifying mood is a credible microbial survival strategy, and he argues that "happy people tend to be more social. And the more social we are, the more chances the microbes have to exchange and spread."

Cut the laminated dough into twelve 12cm (4½-inch) squares. This sliced dough will need to prove overnight. To make sure it stays soft, pop the trays into the oven overnight with a large tray of boiling water at the bottom and the oven light on (if you live in a cooler climate). As the water cools, the steam condenses inside the oven. This will keep the conditions warm and humid, turning your oven into a proving box.

The next day, the slices should have doubled in size. (If they have not, simply wait until they have. It could take up to another 8 hours. This is a slow process; remember, you're working with wild yeast!) Remove them from the oven proving box and preheat the oven to 180°C/350°F/Gas Mark 4 (for best results, use a fan oven).

Just before baking, gently brush the slices with the egg wash, being careful not to knock out the air, and scatter over the sweet Dukkha. Bake in the middle of the oven for 15–18 minutes, until they are a light caramel color. Cool on a wire rack. Once cool, spread Crème pâtissière over each slice. Top with the figs and toasted walnuts and drizzle with honey. Serve immediately. These should be eaten the day they are baked.

# Miso prune Danish

**THE GUT FACTOR** PRUNES ARE HIGH IN FIBRE AND CONTAIN
A WIDE VARIETY OF PREBIOTICS
**SUGGESTED BOTANICAL BLEND** NO. 1: HYBRID
**PROBIOTIC** RAW HONEY

These slices are a simple pleasure for both you and your microbes. The light, buttery layers are made with a fermented dough, making it easier to digest and deliciously complex in flavor. Prunes are dried plums, and are generally perceived to have a laxative effect. Perhaps this isn't the thing you want to think about when you are eating this delicious bake, but consider this: what you feed yourself has an effect, not just on your waist line, but also potentially on the composition and balance of your gut microbiota. Prunes are high in fibre and contain a wide variety of prebiotics, including hemicellulose, pectin and cellulose.

Mix together the filling ingredients in a bowl. Cover and leave on the worksurface overnight to ferment.

The next day, roll out the pastry. It is easier to roll it out in 2 smaller sheets, so cut the block in half and roll each one out into a rectangle measuring 24 x 34cm (9½ x 13½ inches). Spread half the prunes over each pastry sheet. Roll up the pastry lengthways into sausages. Make 5 even marks on each roll, then cut with a very sharp, serrated knife. This will give you 12 Danish.

Line 2 baking trays with baking parchment and transfer the Danish to the trays, giving them plenty of room to expand. Prove overnight at 25—26°C (77—79°F). You can achieve this by placing them in the oven with a warm tray of water at the bottom and the oven light on. This turns your oven into a mini proving box.

In the morning they should have doubled in size. If they haven't, leave them for longer as it can take a while to rise.

When you're ready, preheat the oven to 180°C/350°F/Gas Mark 4. Brush the pastries with egg wash and bake for 18–20 minutes until golden.

Remove from the oven and let cool on the tray for a few moments before transferring to a wire rack. Glaze the pastries with the honey as they cool. These will keep for up to 1 day, but are nicest eaten right away.

---

▶ **STARTER** SWEET

▶ **FOR THE DOUGH**

1 x batch Laminated dough (page 170), but use
   5g salt instead of 10g
1 beaten egg, for egg wash

▶ **FOR THE FILLING**

240g dried prunes, chopped
130g miso paste
2–3 tablespoons water

▶ **TO FINISH**

Raw, unpasteurized honey, to glaze

▶ **PROVING TEMPERATURE** 25°C (77°F)

▶ **SCHEDULE**

| | | |
|---|---|---|
| Day 1 | 8am | Refresh starter (first build) |
| | 9pm | Refresh starter (second build) |
| Day 2 | 8am | Refresh starter (third build) |
| | 10pm | Make leaven |
| Day 3 | 8am | Mix dough and prove at room temperature for 10 hours |
| | 6pm | Transfer to fridge and leave overnight. Prepare your filling ingredients and leave to ferment overnight |
| Day 4 | 8am | Laminate the dough and refrigerate |
| | 8pm | Prepare the Danish and prove overnight |
| Day 5 | 9am | Bake |

# Mille-feuille

**THE GUT FACTOR** POTENTIAL FOR COGNITIVE PROTECTION
AND REDUCED INFLAMMATION. HIGH LEVELS OF PROBIOTICS.
**SUGGESTED BOTANICAL BLEND** NO. 1: HYBRID
**PROBIOTIC** CRÈME PÂTISSIÈRE

▶ **STARTER** SWEET

▶ **FOR THE LEAVEN**

30g wholegrain flour or your chosen Botanical
blend (pages 55–57)
34g water at 30°C
11g triple-refreshed sweet starter (page 110)

▶ **FOR THE DOUGH**

370g Botanical blend no. 1 (page 55), or 270g
strong white roller-milled flour with 100g
stoneground wholegrain
70g sweet butter
150g water
7g salt

▶ **FOR THE LAMINATION**

250g sweet butter

▶ **FOR THE FILLING**

Crème pâtissière (page 75)
500–600g blueberries, or other berries of
your choice

▶ **DDT** 24°C (75°F)

▶ **SCHEDULE** See overleaf

This is a game changer. This is fermented, semi-wholegrain laminated pastry, with a live probiotic crème pâtissière filled with polyphenol-rich blueberries. It is a gut feast.

Blueberries have long been associated with reduced inflammation. And it's not just because they are a good source of fibre, vitamin K and vitamin C. They are especially rich in antioxidant and anti-inflammatory polyphenols that have benefits for our body's cells, support communities of probiotic bacteria in the gut microbiome and, importantly, may be particularly beneficial for brain health and mood. To study how these berries affect brain health, scientists tend to dilute freeze-dried powdered blueberries in a beverage, which allows them to administer high quantities. One study showed that using powdered wild blueberries could improve mood in children and young adults. Another study demonstrated that blueberries could enhance blood flow to the brain, enhancing neural response in older adults with mild dementia.

Make the leaven by mixing together the flour, water and starter. Stir, cover and leave at an ambient temperature for 3 hours.

When you're ready to mix the dough, combine the flour, butter, water and salt in a large mixing bowl until all the ingredients are incorporated. Add the leaven and mix again until the dough comes together. This is a firm dough and there's no need to develop the gluten, but make sure the ingredients are very well mixed. Cover the bowl with a damp dish towel and leave on the kitchen worksurface overnight at ambient temperature.

The next morning, turn the dough out onto your worksurface and roll it out into a measuring rectangle about 35 x 25cm (14 x 10 inches). Cover and put into the fridge to chill until it is 5°C (41°F). It needs to be cold to laminate.

Next, laminate the dough according to the instructions on page 171. Once the dough is laminated, do not cut. Simply roll it out to a 25 x 25cm (10 x 10-inch) square and leave in the fridge overnight.

The next day, preheat your oven to 190°C/375°F/Gas Mark 5. Grease and line 2 baking trays with greased baking parchment.

▶ SCHEDULE

Day 1  10am  Refresh starter (first build)

10pm  Refresh starter (second build)

Day 2  10am  Refresh starter (third build)

6pm  Make leaven

9pm  Mix dough

Day 3  8am  Roll out dough

1pm  Laminate dough

2pm  Laminate dough

3pm  Laminate dough

7pm  Roll out dough and prepare Crème pâtissière. Leave the dough to prove overnight in the fridge, and the Crème pâtissière to ferment

Day 4  9am  Cut into equal pieces and bake Once cool, slice laterally and decorate

Remove the dough from the fridge and carefully slice it into 10 even-sized pieces, each about 5cm x 12.5cm (2 x 5 inches). Transfer these slices to the baking tray.

Bake for 16–18 minutes, then reduce the heat to 160°C/325°F/Gas Mark 3 and bake for another 5 minutes. Remove from the oven and transfer to a wire rack to cool.

The slices will have puffed up significantly in the oven. Using a sharp knife, carefully cut each one in half laterally to give you a top and a bottom.

Fill a pastry bag with Crème pâtissière.

Take 3 pieces of pastry for each Mille-feuille. Pipe 1 piece with Crème pâtissière and add a layer of fruit on top. Take the second piece of pastry and pipe a small blob of Crème pâtissière onto the bottom. Use this to stick the pastry on top. Repeat to create 10 Mille-feuille.

Once assembled, these are best eaten right away.

❱ **STARTER** SWEET

❱ **FOR ALL DOUGHNUT VARIATIONS**

**For the leaven**
75g your chosen Botanical blend (pages 55–57)
90g water at 34°C
35g triple-refreshed Sweet starter (page 110)

**For frying**
1.5 litres (2½ pints) sunflower oil, for frying
100g coconut sugar
1 teaspoon ground cinnamon or powdered vanilla,
   or ½ teaspoon ground cardamom

❱ **SCHEDULE**

| | | |
|---|---|---|
| Day 1 | 8pm | Refresh starter (first build) |
| Day 2 | 8am | Refresh starter (second build) |
| | 8pm | Refresh starter (third build) |
| Day 3 | 8am | Make leaven |
| | 11am | Mix dough |
| | Midday | Bulk for 6 hours at 26°C |
| | 6pm | Put in the fridge at 5°C overnight |
| Day 4 | 8am | Take out of fridge and leave on side for 1 hour to come to room temperature |
| | 9am | Scale and shape |
| | 9:30am | Prove in box at 26°C |
| | 3/4pm | Fry, cool and then fill |

❱ **DDT** 26°C (79°F)

❱ **RASPBERRY & VANILLA DONUTS**

**Diversity Score:** Ingredients 7 + Botanical blend
   18+ = 25+
Ingredients for leaven and for frying (see above)
500g Botanical Blend No. 1 (page 55)
110g water, plus an additional 10–20g if needed
3 large eggs, plus 1 yolk, at room temperature
seeds scraped from 1 fresh vanilla bean
10g salt
100g butter, cubed and softened (at room
   temperature)
100g white sugar

❱ **TO SERVE**
Cultured cream (page 72) and raspberry Fresh
   fruit compote (page 83)
Coconut sugar, to dust (optional)

# Live sourdough donuts

**THE GUT FACTOR** THIS IS THE ULTIMATE DOUGHNUT. ONE THAT IS GOOD FOR YOU AND YOUR MICROBES, BECAUSE IT HAS IT ALL: DIVERSITY, POLYPHENOLS AND BENEFICIAL LIVE PROBIOTICS
**SUGGESTED BOTANICAL BLEND** BLEND NO.1
(WITH YOUR CHOICE OF BLENDS NO. 3–9, SEE PAGES 56–57)
**PROBIOTIC** CRÈME PÂTISSIÈRE, CULTURED CREAM, FRESH FRUIT COMPOTE

Here I have reimagined donuts for optimal gut nourishment. Using a Botanical blend instantly increases levels of fibre and diversity. The long, slow fermentation increases bioavailability of nutrients and resistant starch. But perhaps the ultimate addition is the generous, probiotic-rich fermented fillings, such as the Cultured cream and the fermented live Crème pâtissière with polyphenol-rich Fresh fruit compotes. Instead of Crème pâtissière, you could also use Diplomat cream (see page 75). The acidity of the fruit compote cuts though the rich filling, the chocolate ones are full of flavonoids and pumpkin offers high levels of beta-carotenoids.

## Make the leaven
Make the leaven by mixing together the flour, water and starter. Stir, cover and leave at an ambient temperature for 2 hours.

## Mix
When you are ready to mix your dough, mix together the leaven and all the ingredients for your chosen dough, using a stand mixer, except the butter and sugar (because it interferes with gluten development). The initial mix is to bring the dough together, so use a medium speed for about 4–5 minutes. Now increase the speed to high for 3–4 minutes; this mix is to develop the gluten. It is absolutely essential to develop the gluten before the sugar can be added. You will hear the sound of the mixer change as the dough slams against the side of the bowl. Add the butter, a few cubes at a time, still mixing. Once the butter is fully incorporated, turn off the mixer and let the dough rest for 5 minutes to let the gluten relax. You will see that the dough will be shiny.

After 5 minutes, do the windowpane test. With slightly wet hands, take an egg-sized piece of dough and gently spread it between your fingers. It will feel soft and silky and, as you pull it, it should stretch. If the gluten is strong enough, it will become transparent and you will be able to see light through it, hence the name "windowpane". If it doesn't pass this test, mix the dough for another couple of minutes and repeat. Finally, add the sugar, a little at a time, and mix until incorporated.

## ▶ CHOCOLATE, HAZELNUT & RYE DONUTS

**Diversity Score:** Ingredients 9 + Botanical blend
18+ = 27+

Ingredients for leaven and for frying (see page 181)

400g Botanical blend no. 1

50g wholegrain rye flour

110g water at 16°C/60°F (you may need an
additional 20–30g water to adjust the hydration,
as cocoa can make the dough very stiff and
this will result in a closed crumb structure)

50g unsweetened chocolate powder

5g roasted barley malt

3 large eggs, plus 1 yolk, at room temperature

10g salt

100g butter, cubed and softened (at room
temperature)

100g white sugar

**To serve**

Crème pâtissière (page 75)

Chocolate, almond & hazelnut spread (page 96)

## ▶ CARROT & APRICOT DONUTS

**Diversity Factor:** Ingredients 7 + Botanical blend
18+ = 25+

Ingredients for leaven and for frying (see page 181)

500g Botanical blend no. 1

100g water, plus an additional 10–20g if needed

100g carrots, grated and drained

3 large eggs, plus 1 yolk, at room temperature

10g salt

100g butter, cubed and softened (at room
temperature)

**To serve**

Cultured cream (page 72)

apricot Fresh fruit compote (page 83)

Tips If your leaven is too old, it will
prevent the gluten from forming. Taste your
leaven before using it; it should be slightly
acidic and smell yogurty and lightly tangy.

If your compote is too thin, mix 1 tablespoon
cornstarch with some water to make a
slurry. Add this to the compote in a saucepan.
Stir over a low heat and bring to the boil to
thicken. Allow to cool before using.

Bulk Transfer the dough to a lightly greased bowl and cover with a damp dish towel. Temperature is essential; the dough needs to prove at 26°C (79°F). To achieve this, you will need to use a proving box or, if you don't have one, place in the oven with a warm tray of water in the bottom and the oven light on—this will turn your oven into a proving box. In the first hour, give the dough two full folds about 30 minutes apart: lift and fold the dough gently in half, then turn, lift and fold it again. Leave for half an hour and repeat the folding. This will create layers in your dough. Cover and leave to prove in the fridge overnight.

Scale and shape The next day the dough should have stiffened up. Leave it for an hour on the side, then scale and shape. Lightly dust 2 baking trays with flour. Divide the dough into 18 pieces of about 65g each. Lightly dust your hands with flour, but do not dust the worksurface. Using an open, cupped hand, roll the dough on the worksurface, one piece at a time, to shape. Your hand should move clockwise and, using the worksurface to create resistance, the dough should move in the opposite direction. Do not squash the dough with the palm of your hand; use your fingertips to tuck the dough under, in conjunction with the heel of the hand that create tension.

Transfer the donuts onto the prepared trays, giving them space to double in size without touching. Cover in plastic wrap and transfer to the proving box/oven at 26°C (79°F) to prove for another 6 hours.

Fry Have everything in place before you begin frying. Make sure you have a slotted spoon and plenty of paper towels to hand. Mix the coconut sugar and your chosen spice together on a plate. In a large pan, heat the oil to 180°C (356°F). Too cold, and your donuts will get heavy and oily; too hot; and you will burn the outside and have raw dough in the middle. I increase the temperature by a few degrees when they first go into the oil, then drop the heat as they cook.

Add two or three donuts to the hot oil at a time. They take about 2 minutes and you will need to turn them halfway through cooking. They should expand and be golden brown. Remove with a slotted spoon, gently tap the spoon on the side of the pan to remove excess oil, and pop on paper towels briefly before tumbling into the sugar. Toss generously, transfer to a wire rack to cool, and repeat with the remaining donuts.

Fill Once completely cool, they are ready to fill. You will need about 15–20g of filling for each donut. Fill a pastry bag with the different fillings. A long, pointy pastry tube is an advantage, as you will need to gently push the pastry tube into the donuts. You will need about 15–20g (½–¼oz) of both compote and cream for each one.

# Equipment

**Brioche mould** useful to have if you want to get the authentic shape.

**Crock pots with lids** for keeping your sourdough starter in. It's useful to have two pots, one in use and one washed out and ready to transfer the starter into when the first needs a wash.

**Dish towels**—large dish towels are invaluable to rinse in warm water, wring out and used to cover your mixing bowl during bulk proving. This helps maintain dough temperature and stops it from drying out.

**Dough scraper** a scraper is an inexpensive piece of equipment, but one that makes a huge difference to your baking experience. It makes handling dough and shaping so much easier... it's also handy for cleaning up the work surface after dough preparation.

**Dough cutter** use a stainless-steel cutter for cleanly dividing dough into portions. Choose one with a handle that will be comfortable to use.

**Dutch oven** this is a covered earthenware or cast-iron baking pot for baking breads, but I often bake my 20cm (8-inch) round tin cakes in mine. Keeping the lid on at the start of the bake gets a good rise from your cakes and prevents them from drying out or catching in the heat. Not all tins will fit in, so use when the appropriate tin fits taking the rise of the cake into consideration.

**Flour bin** a large storage jar or flour bin with a lid is useful for keeping flour dry and free of dirt.

**Flour sifter** makes dusting your work surface with flour while kneading so much cleaner, and saves having to put a dough-covered hand into the bag of flour.

**Greaseproof paper** I use this in all my bakes, with butter on and often scattered with a Diversity muesli mix to increase diversity score and to prevent sticking.

**Kitchen timer** if you're busy, it's all too easy to forget your bake, so a good timer is invaluable.

**Cake and loaf tins** heavy duty, non-stick tins will turn out good bakes every time. Having a couple of tins of different sizes adds to the variety of cakes you can bake.

**Measuring jug** a glass measuring jug is useful for mixing hot and cold water to get the temperature right for mixing dough.

**Measuring spoons** for accurate measuring of small amounts.

**Mini muffin tin** For the Cherry bites on page 167.

**Large mixing bowl** a beautiful vintage, stoneware mixing bowl is a joy to use. The older ones tend to be bigger and a good large bowl gives you plenty of space to make dough without ending up with flour all over the worksurface and floor, so it is better to choose a bowl that's bigger than you think you'll need.

**Small mixing bowl** useful for mixing leaven to leave overnight for the next day's dough.

**A folder** I like to keep records of everything from measurements, temperatures and timings to the results of each bake. This helps me to make small changes for next time.

**Oven mitts** essential for taking hot cakes from in the oven.

**Pasta machine** for the pappardelle on page 131.

**Pastry bag and tube** for piping sourdough kisses (page 141) and jalebi (page 142).

**Scales** an accurate set of scales is a must for consistent results. Digital scales are easy to use. Choose some that measure increments down to 1g for weighing out small amounts of salt. There are scales which allow you to weigh in baker's percentages, cutting out the need for back of an envelope calculations when you want to change recipe proportions.

**Rolling pin** essential. Choose a heavy, wide one.

**Thermometer** temperature has a huge impact on fermentation and can be controlled in a number of ways. Ensure the water you use to make the dough (to get your DDT) is at the right temperature by using a basic food thermometer.

**Wire rack** for cooling. It doesn't need to be anything fancy.

**Wax cloths** see resources, page 187.

# Resources

**The Sourdough Club** In conjunction with the Sourdough School book, and this Sweet Sourdough book we have an active online sourdough club, with tutorials, videos, an active forum and a community of sourdough bakers. You are able to apply for a discount code if you have bought a copy of any of Vanessa's books.
www.thesourdoughclub.com

**Atlas Biomed** are currently collaborating on my studies. We believe they are the world's leading gut microbial testing company. We absolutely love the way they present the test findings, and then use these to make specific food recommendations which help people nurture the positive bacteria within their gut.
www.atlasbiomed.com/uk

**Mock Mill** is a company developing and selling a range of grain mills and accessories. The great thing is that they make home milling accessible to all bakers, so everyone can enjoy the flavor and the experience of baking with freshly milled flour.
www.mockmill.com/eu

# Online resources

**Bakery Bits** I have worked with Bakery Bits for over a decade. We collaborate with them regularly and love their range of baking ingredients and equipment.
www.bakerybits.co.uk

**Bimuno** is a dietary fibre supplement that has been shown to help maintain good gut health by supporting the Bifidobacterial population. It has been tested in clinical trials and shown to compare favorably to both similar products and probiotic yogurts in its beneficial effect on the gut microbes.
www.bimuno.com

**Doves Farm** is another of the mills whose organic flours we use regularly at The Sourdough School.
www.dovesfarm.co.uk

**Foricher** for flours that are grown and milled in France. This incredible French flour is blended with several varieties of grain at the mill. www.foricher.com/en

**Gilchesters Organics** I absolutely love the range of flours and grains from this family-run farm and mill in the northeast of England. They grow carefully selected heritage grains with an emphasis on traditional farming methods to build healthy soils and care for the environment. www.gilchesters.com

**Marriage's** is one of my favourite white bread flours to blend with. They offer a range of organic flours and I use their organic bread flour for Blend No 1.
www.flour.co.uk

**Planet Organic** is an innovative company with a fantastic range of organic products. This is where we source most of the dried ingredients we use on our courses, especially nuts and seeds. We love everything about this store, from their focus on natural, sustainable and, where possible, British products to their commitment to reducing packaging and encouraging a healthy lifestyle.
www.planetorganic.com

**Puratos** The research we do here at The Sourdough School and the backbone of my work wouldn't be possible without some financial support. So, we are sponsored by and work with Puratos, the leading providers of lactic acid bacteria and yeast to the manufacturing industry. Our philosophy here at the school is that the discussion has to be around every aspect of sourdough, not simply artisan or handmade bakes. It has to go beyond sourdough being a fashionable food to looking at how we can change the manufacturing system of our most basic of foods and embrace the health benefits of sourdough. We are absolutely delighted to be sponsored by Puratos—without their contribution, this research simply couldn't be done here, and this knowledge needs to reach all baked goods. www.puratos.com

**Riverford** I've been using Riverford for many years. It is a well-known organic vegetable box scheme, delivering fresh produce across the UK. Although many of the vegetables and fruit we use in our baking are freshly picked from the garden here at the school, we regularly supplement our own harvests with produce from Riverford. We fully support their mission to encourage and enable good farming practices, and to make connections between the farmer and consumer—everyone should know where the food on their plate comes from! www.riverford.co.uk

**Rude Health** is amazing. We use the Rude Health porridges in many of our bakes. www.rudehealth.com

**Sharpham Park** is our wonderful supplier of spelt grain. Roger Saul grows the organic spelt at his farm in Somerset and mills the grain using traditional methods. The farm is also home to a herd of red deer, along with hedgerows and field margins planted to provide food and shelter for local wildlife. www.sharphampark.com

**Symprove** is a probiotic with clinical evidence that it helps gut-friendly colonize the digestive system, which leads to many potential health benefits. One of the things that is really important to us is not just talking about the health claims for fermented foods and supplements but knowing that these claims have been scientifically tested and proven. www.symprove.com

**Toast** The workwear I use on a daily basis and throughout this book has been produced through a collaboration with Toast. We use their aprons, denim and workwear here at the school. Because it's not simply about looking good, it's also a question of integrity. We love working with a British company that supports other artisan makers and makes clothes that are designed to last. They wash beautifully too! www.toa.st/u

# Main glossary

**Bulk** Bulk fermentation is the first rise/fermentation before the dough is scaled or divided into and shaped.

**DDT** Desired Dough Temperature—the temperature of your dough acts as an accelerator, controlling the speed of fermentation. Keeping your dough to the desired temperature recommended in each recipe will give you better and more consistent results. See page 120.

**Dough rheology** Rheology is the study of the way that liquid, solid or semi-solid materials react to pressure. So dough rheology is the way the dough behaves, for example how elastic it is or how strong is.

**Hygroscopic** A hygroscopic substance is one that readily attracts water, for example through absorption.

**Maillard reaction** this is a reaction between amino acids and sugars when heated that results in browning and an intensification of flavors. It happens when we toast bread, for example.

**Microbiome v microbiota** "Gut microbiome" and "gut microbiota" are often used interchangeably, but these two terms have subtle differences. The gut microbiome refers to the collection of genomes of all the microorganisms in the gut. Gut microbiota actually refers to specific microorganisms that are found within the gut.

**Osmotolerant** an osmotolerant starter will tolerate osmosis (it will tolerate water being drawn out). Sugar is hydroscopic, meaning it draws out water, which slows down fermentation. During the process of building and refreshing your sweet starter, you effectively train it to cope with sugar and its hygroscopic effects.

**Population wheat** An approach to growing wheat that reintroduces diversity back into the fields by creating what is known as a 'population wheat'. This is a genetically diverse crop produced by sowing and number of different varieties of wheat together, then harvesting and using this seed to sow again next year.

# Ingredient glossary

**Banana flour** this is a flour made of dried green bananas. It is gluten-free and a source of resistant starch.

**Ndali vanilla powder** this is my preferred way to add vanilla flavoring. Ndali vanilla powder is made from the entire vanilla bean, ground into a powder, with no additives.

**Raw, unpasteurized honey** raw honey is a probiotic, but loses its rawness at more than 30°C. This means that, if the honey is heated, it's no longer a probiotic, so we try to avoid heating it wherever possible to retain maximum benefit. People receiving immunotherapy and pregnant people should refer to medical guidelines on raw honey.

**Maca powder** this is the dried, ground root of the maca plant (a cruciferous vegetable). It has a strong nutritional profile and is high in antioxidants.

**Spraymalt** this is a dried malt extract. It adds a lovely, malty flavor and can give a subtle sweetness.

# Alternative equipment & ingredients

**Wax cloths** A lot of bakers use plastic wrap to cover their dough while it proves, but at the School we try to avoid using plastic wrap whenever possible. Although I do use a wet dish towel to cover my dough from time to time, I find the most effective method is to use a wax cloth. You can find instructions on how to make your own on my website: www.sourdough.co.uk/make-wax-cloth-sourdough/

**Vegan alternatives** Chia egg—if you are vegan, you can replace eggs with chia seeds and water. Substitute each egg with 1 tablespoon chia seeds mixed with 3 tablespoons water. We've tested all our recipes with a chia egg to make sure everyone can enjoy them.

To use these QR codes with an Android Phone, launch your camera, point it at the QR code, and tap to use the code.

For more information on sourdough research:

To apply for a discount for the online Sourdough Club:

To buy the Atlas Biomed gut microbiome test:

To buy a Mockmill professional grain mill:

# Index

# Index

# Acknowledgments

A sourdough starter is a community. It is a co-operative of microorganisms that co-exist, each one having a role. Likewise, a book is not written, it is created. It evolves. Saying thank you never seems quite enough, so to the following people, know that you inspired, supported, cajoled, baked, criticized, tested, retested, perfected, photographed, proofread, baked, ate, and without your input this book would not be what it is: the thoughts, flavors, energy, passion, and love on my mind bound in a book.

My incredible Sourdough School team, Lucy, Faye, Jo, Georgia, Emma, Bran, and Sarah and Miguel—my baking family. A huge thank you particularly to Sarah Smith. To Michael James, you are amazing. I can't thank you enough for your warmth, knowledge, and contribution to this book.

The amazing Kyle team, Jenny Dye and especially Judith. Tara O'Sullivan for getting the details out of my head and on to paper and Nassima—it's a feeling and you capture the essence of each bake so beautifully. You are an extraordinary team.

My testers, a team of 20—I am beyond grateful for your time and input, but in particular Christine, Chris, Ian, Ann, Shirley, Claudia, Debra, Linda, David, Catherine, Jon, and Piotr—Bread Pete. A huge thank you to Karl De Smedt, the sourdough librarian, for testing all the scheduling and advanced bakes. To my brilliant research team, Leigh-Ann Stewart and Sarah Smith.

Dayna Brackley for your advice and friendship and to Alice Den Boer for your amazing friendship and incredible support.

Gilchesters, to both Bille and Andrew for knowledge and support, and John Letts, Michael the Baker, Josiah from Hodmedods for friendship and conversation, and Edward Dickin for barley.

Thank you to my gorgeous baking brothers Richard Hart, Gabriel Bonci, Andrei George, and Adam Pagor for the inspiration, laugher and love. Thank you doesn't cover it—you are family and I absolutely love you to bits. To Sergey and the Atlas Biomed Team and Stefan Capelle, and Karl of Puratos for your belief in my work and your support have made it possible to reshape our understanding of sourdough.

To Tim Spector, for your vision and your support—because now the world makes sense.

# Afterword

### Sharing a journey to better health

The word "commensalism" is derived from the word "commensal", meaning "eating at the same table" in human social interaction, which in turn comes through French from the Medieval Latin commensalis, meaning "sharing a table" or "sharing a meal", which is exactly what we do when we eat: we share a meal with tens of trillions of microorganisms, including at least 1000 different species of known bacteria that inhabit our gut. As mind-blowing as that is, the relationship between you, your sourdough, and your microbiome gets even more intimate. You may be following the same recipe and using the same ingredients as another baker in another country miles away from you, but the diversity of the microbes in that loaf, that pancake, or that cultured butter will be unique to you, based on the microbial community that inhabits your kitchen and the skin in your hands. I hope this book is just the beginning of that realization that whenever you're touching your sourdough, you are engaging in a beautiful dialogue with your microbes, who will be with you on your journey of discovery of new flavors and textures as well as, hopefully, in a journey to better health.

**Miguel Toribio-Mateas**, Nutritional Neuroscience Research Fellow at London South Bank University and The Sourdough School in-house Nutritionist